Vera
Lex

Journal of the International Natural Law Society

New Series Volume 4, Numbers 1&2   Winter 2003

COPYRIGHT © 2003
PACE UNIVERSITY PRESS
1 PACE PLAZA
NEW YORK, NY 10038

ISBN 0-944473-65-2

CONTRIBUTORS
Address all submissions and correspondence to The Editor, VERA LEX, Pace University, Department of Philosophy & Religious Studies, 1 Pace Plaza, New York, NY 10038. Please send two copies of the paper submitted. Include adequate margins, double space everything (text, notes, works cited, quotations). Use U.S. spelling and punctuation style, (e.g. periods inside quotation marks; "double quotes" for opening and closing quotations). The University of Chicago Manual of Style, 13th Edition, is to be consulted regarding matters of style. Notes are to be numbered consecutively (in Arabic numerals) and placed at the bottom of the page.

SUBSCRIBERS
VERA LEX is published annually by Pace University Press, 41 Park Row, Room 1510, New York, NY 10038. Subscription price: $40 for libraries and institutions; $25 for individuals. Please send all subscription inquiries to The Editor.

INDEXING AND ABSTRACTING
VERA LEX is indexed in *Philosopher's Index*.

VERA LEX, the journal of the International Natural Law Society, was established to communicate and dialogue on the subject of natural law and natural right, to introduce natural law philosophy into the mainstream of contemporary thought, and to strengthen the current revived interest in the discussion of morals and law and advance its historical research.

Why do we use a shell (*Nautilus pomplilus Linnaeus*) to symbolize *vera lex*? The logarithmic spiraling and overlapping chambers of the shell are endless. They suggest a patterned development and evolution that, by its radial and circular design, never comes to an end. This means that the shell is at once specific and real, while its form, like law, is abstract and ideal.

The pattern of a shell is, like good law, uniform, regular and reliable. It can therefore be anticipated and known. The pattern of a shell is balanced, like justice. *Una iustitia*.

A shell is a biological being. Like law, it has life and dynamic. It grows. (There is an average of thirty growth lines per chamber, one for every day in the lunar cycle, suggesting that a new chamber is put down each lunar month and a new growth line each day, thus recording two different natural rhythms, lunar and solar.)

The shell is a universal and common object known to everyone. A shell is not soft tissue easily destroyed. And yet, like liberty, it is fragile in certain respects if stepped on with an iron boot. It has to be guarded with vigilance or it is crushed.

In every shell lives a nautilus. If the shell is law, the nautilus (snail) is a person—it is alive—person and law. Their destinies, like person and law, are interdependent.

Vera
Lex

leges innumerae, una iustitia

CONTENTS

NEW SERIES VOLUME 4, NUMBERS 1 & 2   WINTER 2003

INTRODUCTION

NATURAL LAW THEORY AND FEMINISM
Lori Alward

A theme in this issue of *Vera Lex* is the relationship between natural law theory and feminist theory. At first blush, it might seem that the two theories are deeply incompatible. Indeed, both Nancy Snow and Shelby Weitzel, whose articles appear in this issue, argue that at least some versions of natural law theory and feminist theory are incompatible, but each also argues that at least some versions are compatible or could be made more compatible. Whether this is so has been discussed in some recent works of feminist philosophy and theology. For example, Christine Pierce argues that natural law theory is antithetical to feminism in her recent book, *Immovable Laws, Irresistible Rights: Natural Law, Moral Rights, and Feminist Ethics*. In contrast, in *Feminist Ethics and Natural Law: The End of Anathemas*, Cristina Traina argues that feminist ethics needs natural law theory. Which side of this issue one comes down on depends largely on what one is willing to count as natural law theory. If natural law must be confined to a kind of classical Aristotelian theory, such as Thomism, one might conclude that natural law theory is inherently incompatible with feminist theory and practice. On the other hand, if one is willing to include in the category of natural law theory a neoaristotelian theory, such as Martha Nussbaum's capabilities theory, or a contemporary Kantian theory, such as some versions of liberal feminist jurisprudence, then it appears that at least some types of feminist theory are compatible, and in fact, some theories, such as Nussbaum's, are versions of natural law theory. The annotated bibliography, which catalogues works relevant to this theme, was created to reflect the broader conception of natural law theory, and also indicates the breadth and richness of recent scholarly work in this area.

In her article, "Feminism and Natural Law Theory: Irreconcilable Differences?" Nancy Snow argues that it is difficult to address directly the question whether feminism and natural law theory are compatible since there are so many versions of each theory that it is difficult to find convergence within each theory, let alone across the theories. So rather than compare the theories, Snow compares central figures within each tradition—Virginia Held and Thomas Aquinas—and examines what each philosopher says about a key issue, practical reason. Snow finds similarities between the two views: for example, both Held and Aquinas believe that the theory is shaped by practice. Nonetheless, despite some similarities, Snow argues, there are deep and serious differences between Held's feminist ethics and Aquinas's natural law theory. Snow gives several reasons for these differences. She argues that Aquinas's methodology is foundationalist and deductive, whereas Held's is coherentist, and that while both theories of practical reason are teleological, in Aquinas, practical reason is restricted to choosing means, since ends are set by God, and in Held's theory, practical reason is used to set ends, as well as to determine what means will be used in pursuit of those ends. Snow concludes that these sorts of theoretical differences are deep and pervasive, and at least appear to be irreconcilable. A further problem with Aquinas's view, of course, is that Aquinas uncritically adopts Aristotle's view of women's inferiority to men. Snow sees this as essential to Aquinas's theory of practical reason, and thus concludes that the theory is incompatible with feminism. Yet Snow does not abandon hope regarding the possibility of convergence between natural law theory and feminism. She believes that convergence might be achieved by modifying certain assumptions within both feminism and natural law theory. Snow points out that theologians have already made this move and urges philosophers to follow their example.

Shelby Weitzel takes on the debate between Christine Pierce and Cristina Traina in her article, "Does Feminism Need Natural Law Like a Fish Needs a Bicycle? Feminism, Autonomy, and the Human Telos." For reasons that would seem eminently sensible to most feminists, Weitzel defends Pierce's attack on the sort of canonical natural law theory that Traina defends. A theory that asserts that birth control is immoral or that homosexuality is unnatural, for example, seems to be antithetical to the aims of feminism, despite Traina's attempts to rescue the theory. Nonetheless, Weitzel does not uncritically defend Pierce's position, since she regards it as construing natural law theory too narrowly. Weitzel agrees that if a Thomistic version of natural law theory is inherently misogynistic, then it is anathema to feminists. But Weitzel offers an alternative to Thomism: Nussbaum's Aristotelian capabilities theory. Traditionalists might object that capabilities theory is not truly a version of natural law theory, since it does not provide what Traina calls a "substantive telos" but instead values the human capacity to set one's own ends. Weitzel argues that this is a virtue of Nussbaum's theory, a claim that Pierce, if not Traina, would certainly agree with.

Finally, this issue also includes an article about H. L. A. Hart's criticism of Austin's command theory of law: "Austin's Complementary Jurisprudence," by Avner Levin. Levin argues that Austin's theory of law was not the extreme version of legal positivism that Hart famously criticizes. He calls Hart's allegedly inaccurate reconstruction of Austin's jurisprudence "Austinism," to distinguish it from Austin's true view, which is "complementary jurisprudence." Austin's complementary theory makes it clear that law has a moral basis, according to Levin.

Levin claims that the widespread acceptance of Hart's criticisms of Austin has led to the belief that Austin's theory is too simplistic and has nothing useful to offer contemporary jurisprudence. However, since Hart's argument against Austin is a straw person, according to Levin, Austin still has much to teach us, and his theory does not present the same practical problems that Austinism does. For example, Austinism tends to oversimplify the structure of law and is consequently unable to distinguish between a sovereign and a dictator or a sanction and a command. Austin's complementary theory, in contrast, has none of these problems. In short, Austin's complementary jurisprudence is far more sophisticated and nuanced than Austinism, as well as having the virtue of recognizing the normative basis of positive law. Ironically, Austin's theory is so rich, according to Levin, that it incorporates elements of some of Austin's most famous critics: Hart, Dworkin, Finnis, and Raz. If Levin is right, of course, he is offering a startling new reading of Austin, which might require resituating Austin within the history of jurisprudence.

FEATURED ARTICLES

FEMINISM AND NATURAL LAW THEORY: IRRECONCILABLE DIFFERENCES?
Nancy Snow

INTRODUCTION

Feminist moral theologians have recently sought to find areas of convergence between feminist ethics and natural law theory.[1] This project faces several difficulties. One problem is perspective. Feminists deliberately place women's issues, experiences, and perspectives at the center of ethics, and criticize historical ethical theories for being gender-biased.[2] Natural law theorists generally do not give women's concerns pride of place, nor is it my impression that they embrace the criticism that traditional Western ethics is gender-biased. Another complicating factor is the sheer number and complexity of views that can count as either "feminist" or "natural law." Perhaps convergence cannot be found within either area of inquiry, much less across both.

Despite these concerns, attempts to find convergence are informative. Such efforts reveal similarities and differences in feminist and natural law approaches and prompt questions about their significance. Progress is best made, I believe, not by surveying the plethora of feminist and natural law views, but instead by concentrating on the work of central figures on fundamental issues. Here I focus on practical reason by considering

---

[1] See, for example, Cristina L. H. Traina, *Feminist Ethics and Natural Law: The End of the Anathemas* (Washington, D.C.: Georgetown University Press, 1999); Lisa Sowle Cahill, *Sex, Gender, and Christian Ethics* (Cambridge, England: Cambridge University Press, 1996); and *Feminist Ethics and the Catholic Moral Tradition*, ed. Charles E. Curran, Margaret A. Farley, and Richard A. McCormick, S. J. (New York/Mahwah, New Jersey: Paulist Press, 1996). For a critique of this approach, especially of Traina, see Christine Pierce, *Immovable Laws, Irresistible Rights: Natural Law, Moral Rights, and Feminist Ethics* (Lawrence, Kansas: University Press of Kansas, 2000), pp. 115-24.

[2] See, for example, Virginia Held, *Feminist Morality: Transforming Culture, Society, and Politics* (Chicago, Illinois: The University of Chicago Press, 1993), pp. 43ff. Aquinas, whose work is discussed here, thinks that women are properly subordinate to men, a view that feminists and others rightly reject. I discuss his claims about women later in the text, but set them aside throughout most of the discussion for the sake of identifying similarities and differences in his and Held's views of practical reason.

feminist moral inquiry as portrayed by Virginia Held in *Feminist Morality: Transforming Culture, Society, and Politics*, and the account of prudence by Thomas Aquinas in the *Summa Theologica*.[3] The work of both thinkers is central to their traditions, and practical reason is key for ethics. Apart from finding common ground, delineating similarities and differences in their views helps to illuminate the purposes of practical reason within their theories as well as the theoretical structures themselves.

HELD ON FEMINIST MORAL INQUIRY

In many ways, Held's discussion summarizes feminist thinking about practical reason, yet its aim is to clarify issues of methodology to guide future inquiry (see 22). She makes plain from the outset the importance of experience and practice to feminist moral inquiry:

> Moral inquiry involves living our lives and actively shaping our relationships with others rather than accurately registering and theorizing about the impressions made upon us by what some take to be an external world. To engage in the development of feminist morality is to seek to improve practices in which knowledge is only one component, though an important

---

[3] See Held; also St. Thomas Aquinas, *Summa Theologica*, Vols. I and II, tr. Fathers of the English Dominican Province (New York: Benziger Brothers, Inc.). The account of prudence is in volume II, II-II, 47-56; relevant also in volume I are I-II, 14, 1-6; I-II, 57, 4-6; 58, 1-5; 61, 1-5; 65, 1; see also St. Thomas Aquinas, *Commentary on Aristotle's Nicomachean Ethics*, tr. C. I. Litzinger, O.P. (Notre Dame, Indiana: Dumb Ox Books, 1993). References to Held and the *Summa* are hereafter made in the body of the text. Prudence is one of the cardinal virtues for Aquinas. Consequently, discussing it as part of his natural law theory might seem odd. There is controversy about how well natural law theory and virtue theory fit together in general as well as within Aquinas's theory. See the discussions by Robert A. Gahl, Jr., "From the Virtue of a Fragile Good to a Narrative Account of Natural Law," *International Philosophical Quarterly*, vol. XXXVII, no. 4, issue no. 148 (December 1997), 99. 457-72; and Russell Hittinger, "Natural Law and Virtue: Theories at Cross Purposes," in Robert P. George, ed., *Natural Law Theory: Contemporary Essays* (Oxford: Clarendon Press, 1992), pp. 42-69; on the role of prudence and natural law in Aquinas, see Daniel Mark Nelson, *The Priority of Prudence: Virtue and Natural Law in Thomas Aquinas and the Implications for Modern Ethics* (University Park, Pennsylvania: The Pennsylvania State University Press, 1992). For reasons stated in the text, I think that Aquinas's theories of natural law, prudence, and virtue are complementary parts of a well-integrated, architectonic theory of morality. See Thomas S. Hibbs, *Virtue's Splendor: Wisdom, Prudence, and the Human Good* (New York: Fordham University Press, 2001); and Maria Carl, "Law, Virtue, and Happiness in Aquinas's Moral Theory," *The Thomist*, vol. 61, no. 3 (July 1997), pp. 425-47.

one. It is to cultivate the art of living a life as admirable for women as for men. (22)

Held's remark about cultivating "the art of living a life as admirable for women as for men" is instructive. It enables us to locate feminist moral inquiry within a philosophical tradition of ethical theorizing that can be viewed, very roughly, as falling into two camps. Theorists such as Plato and Kant are concerned with developing theory to guide practice. We find answers to ethical problems through abstract theorizing. This is a "top-down" approach in which theory shapes the contours of our ethical experiences. We must "fit" our experience to the theory, but not vice-versa. Other philosophers take a more "hands on" approach. Though Aristotle uses abstractions in his theory—for example, he urges us to ask what the virtuous person would do in deciding upon our own actions—the virtuous person is formed through the practical experience of living. Aquinas, too, is deeply concerned with the practical. For each theorist, the virtues in their lived reality, and, for Aquinas, some of the precepts of natural law, are shaped by experience. Their approach is, if not entirely "bottom up," more amenable than the other camp to allowing theory to be shaped by practice. Held's vision of feminist moral inquiry places it firmly within the more "hands on" camp of ethical theorizing.

Further, Held's idea of cultivating the art of living a life sets the stage for a robust conception of practical reasoning that involves far more than propositional knowledge and syllogistic reasoning. She claims that "The central category of feminist thought, at least in its contemporary phase, is experience" (24). Experience is not confined to empirical observation, but is the actual lived experience of emotions and relationships. Moral theories must be tested against this lived experience (see 23).

Within the category of experience, "moral experience" has special significance. She writes:

> *Moral* experience is the experience of consciously choosing to act, or refrain from acting, on grounds by which we are trying conscientiously to be guided. *Moral* experience is the experience of accepting or rejecting moral positions for what we take to be good moral reasons or well-founded moral intuitions or on the basis of what we take to be justifiable moral feelings. *Moral* experience is the experience of approving or disapproving of actions or states of affairs of which we are aware and of

> evaluating the feelings we have and the relationships we are in.
> (24; italics hers)

Moral experience contains a strong emotional component. Moral experience can cause us to re-evaluate and revise independently held moral beliefs and theories (see 25). Held gives the example of how someone might re-evaluate her practice of eating meat and her beliefs about the legitimacy of that practice on the basis of the moral experience of disapproval of factory farming (see 25-27). Revisions in beliefs about meat eating can cause other beliefs and theories to be changed. The picture that emerges is coherentist. Moral experiences include judgments arrived at independently of moral theories. These judgments are brought into coherence with other judgments, and thereby have the potential to effect revisions of a range of beliefs.[4]

The emphasis on experience in feminist moral inquiry suggests an enhanced role for emotion. Feminists see the cultivation of emotions as having a role akin to that emphasized in traditional moral theories: emotions help us to carry out the dictates of reason and set preferences (see 29). However, their role is not only subsidiary to reason. Emotions should also help to form moral understanding and to decide upon the recommendations of morality (see 30). Not all emotions should have this role, however. Held recognizes that some emotions are harmful: "An adequate moral theory should be built on appropriate feelings as well as on appropriate reasoning" (30). Appropriate feelings that feminists value include empathy, caring, love, hopefulness, and indignation in the face of cruelty (see 30-31).

Stressing experience also leads to a focus on relationships, especially relationships that have been excluded from the purview of morality, such as mothering (see 31-33). If one views moral inquiry and reasoning as properly occurring within relationships, several Enlightenment ideals of moral reasoning must be rejected or revised. For example, the ideal of impartiality is jettisoned as the preferred perspective from which all moral issues should be judged. Some moral issues, such as those which arise within the context of particular, personal relationships, should not be approached from an impartial perspective. Thus, the ideal of "impartial

---

[4] Held draws a parallel with Rawls's wide reflective equilibrium, but notes that, unlike Rawls, she believes that judgments based on feelings can and should be included in the judgments among which coherence is sought (see 28).

reason," or the use of reason from an allegedly neutral, impartial perspective, is at least circumscribed as an ethical tool. Abstract principle
must sometimes be subordinated to relationships: "A feminist approach
to morality might give a felt relationship of trust priority over principle
and seek a morality compatible with this priority" (33). Consistent with
this approach is a greater reliance on actual, as opposed to hypothetical
experience (see 34), and skepticism about the value of adopting the perspective of the abstract, rational agent, or the ideal observer, as against
viewing morality from the point of view of actual, embodied persons (see
35).

Feminist moral inquiry is aware of the complexity of context and of
the complex relationship between context and principle (see 40).
Sensitivity to contexts encourages a collaborative approach to moral reasoning. Held quotes Iris Marion Young, who defends a "dialogic conception of normative reason" (41). According to Young, the absence of an
impartial perspective requires that all participants contribute to a dialogue. As long as all perspectives speak freely and are heard, bias and dis-
tortion are avoided (see 41). Dialogic approaches ask "...that we listen to
each other in actual conversations in actual communities" (41).

AQUINAS ON PRUDENCE

Prudence (*prudentia*) is right reason about things to be done; it concerns habits of choice and action (see S. T. I-II, 57, 4; 58, 4-5; 65, 1).
Prudence is also "...wisdom about human affairs..." (S. T. II-II, 47, 2,
reply obj. 1). It resides in the practical reason (see S. T. II-II, 47, 1-2; S.
T. I-II, 57, 4). There can be no moral virtue without prudence, and no prudence without moral virtue (see S. T. I-II, 58, 5). The moral virtues are
unified through prudence (see S. T. I-II, 65,1). Prudence "...applies universal principles to the particular conclusions of practical matters" (S. T.
II-II, 47, 6). Thus, it requires knowledge of both "...universal principles
of reason and the singulars about which actions are concerned" (S. T. II-
II, 47, 3). Prudence does not decide the end of moral virtues, but regulates
the means (see S. T. II-II, 65, 1). It can concern the individual good, the
good of states, the good of households, and military good (see S. T. II-II,
47, 11; II-II, 50, 1-4).

There are three acts of prudence: taking counsel, forming a judgment,
and commanding (see S. T. II-II, 47, 8). Aquinas links counsel with dis-

covery. It is an act of inquiry. Judgment is an act of speculative reason. Command, the chief act of prudence, applies "...to action the things counselled and judged" (S. T. II-II, 47, 8). Aquinas offers an extensive analysis of counsel. It is collaborative: "Counsel properly implies a conference held between several..." (S. T. I-II, 14, 3). The conference is " . . . not of any kind, but about what is to be done..." (S. T. I-II, 14, 3, reply obj. 1). It is also about whatever relates to what is to be done, for example, future events (see S. T. I-II, 14, 3, reply obj. 3). Solicitude, or care in taking counsel, is part of prudence (see S. T. II-II, 47, 9), as is docility, which is the willingness to be "...taught by others, especially by old folk who have acquired a sane understanding of the ends in practical matters" (S. T. II-II, 49, 3).

Specific virtues are associated with prudence: the disposition to take good counsel, or excellence in deliberation (*eubolia*); good judgment about things which are deliberated (*synesis*); and a third, higher form of judgment, which judges matters according to higher principles, "...denotes a certain discrimination in judgment," and deals with issues of justice and equity (*gnome*) (S. T. II-II, 51, 1-4).[5] Specific vices are associated with imprudence and are defects in each of the acts of prudence: precipitation, or not taking proper counsel, either from contempt of taking direction, or rashness (see S. T. II-II, 53, 3, reply obj. 2);[6] thoughtlessness, or "...failure to judge rightly through contempt or neglect of those things on which right judgment depends" (S. T. II-II, 53, 4); and inconstancy, or the failure of reason "...in commanding what has been counselled and judged" (S. T. II-II, 53, 5). Aquinas attributes these vices to lust, since attention to sensible objects, including sexual pleasure, distracts the intellect (see S. T. II-II, 53, 6). Negligence, which is a lack of due solicitude, pertains to imprudence and is a special sin (see S. T. II-II, 54, 1-2).

5 See also Aquinas, *Commentary on Aristotle's Nicomachean Ethics*, pp. 386-93.

6 Aquinas believes that taking good counsel consists in following the "steps" of prudence. One follows these steps by an orderly progression through the quasi-integral parts of prudence: "...memory of the past, intelligence of the present, shrewdness in considering the future outcome, reasoning which compares one thing with another, docility in accepting the opinions of others" (S. T. II-II, 53, 3). Precipitation is rushing into action without taking these steps (see S. T. II-II, 53, 3).

Other parts of prudence (called "quasi-integral parts") are: memory, understanding, docility, shrewdness, reason, foresight, circumspection, and caution (see S. T. II-II, 49, 1- 8). Some of these terms are used technically and require explanation. Memory is clear enough. "Understanding" is used technically to refer to "...the right estimate about some final principle, which is taken as self-evident..." (S. T. II-II, 49, 2) Since every deduction of reason proceeds from principles, understanding is crucial (see S. T. II-II, 49, 2). Docility is explained above. "Shrewdness" is defined as "...an easy or rapid conjecture in finding the middle term..." (S. T. II-II, 49, 4). "Reason" refers to reasoning ability (see S. T. II-II, 49, 5). Aquinas explains "foresight" by saying that future contingents are the matter of prudence, and since foresight looks ahead to something distant and directs the present toward it, foresight is a part of prudence (see S. T. II-II, 49, 6). "Circumspection" is "...comparing the means with the circumstances" (S. T. II-II, 49, 7). Since evil is mingled with good, Aquinas asserts that prudence requires caution, which enables us to " . . . have such a grasp of good as to avoid evil" (S. T. II-II, 49, 8).

As an intellectual virtue, prudence is not in us by nature, but is acquired by teaching and experience (see S. T. II-II, 47,15). Though not in us by nature, prudence has several important connections with the natural law. First, prudence is knowledge about the means to be taken to attain the fixed ends of human life. These ends are goods; we have natural inclinations to pursue them; some people have virtues that incline them to these ends; and consequently, naturally right judgment about them (see S. T. II-II, 47,15). Indeed, the natural inclinations that rational creatures have to their proper acts and ends are the natural law; this is the rational creature's participation in the eternal law (see S. T. II-II, 91, 2). Thus, prudence enables us to take the means necessary to fulfill the precepts of the natural law. But the means, "...far from being fixed, are of manifold variety according to the variety of persons and affairs" (S. T. II-II, 47, 15). Consequently, knowledge of the means does not arise in us naturally, though some persons are naturally better disposed than others to discern them (see S. T. II-II, 47, 15).

Prudence also enables us to choose the means necessary to achieve the ends of the moral virtues (see S. T. II-II, 47, 6), and is, consequently, connected with the natural law insofar as the natural law prescribes the acts of the virtues. All acts of the virtues are prescribed by the natural law insofar as everyone has the natural inclination to act according to reason (see S. T. II-II, 94, 3).

Finally, prudence requires knowledge of universal practical principles (see S. T. II-II, 47, 15). According to Aquinas, the universal principles of both speculative and practical reason are known naturally, as is true of the primary, more general principles; or are "...not inherited from nature..." but are acquired by discovery through experience or teaching, as is true of the secondary, more determinate principles (S. T. II-II, 47, 15). Some of these principles of practical reason are precepts of natural law (see S. T. II-II, 94, 2; 4). Aquinas's theory of prudence, of the moral and intellectual virtues, and of the natural law form a seamless web: a comprehensive, well-integrated theory of moral life that spans the public and private spheres.

SIMILARITIES AND DIFFERENCES

Here I compare and contrast Held and Aquinas on six points: experience, context, the role of principles, emotion, relationship, and collaboration.

Experience, context, and the role of principles are related issues. Each theorist takes experience seriously, and this has implications for their views on context and the role of principle. Held stresses experience as a general category of feminist thought, and takes pains to define moral experience. Aquinas repeatedly emphasizes prudence's concern with choice and action, with means to ends, and with practical affairs across a range of enterprises. The lived reality of the virtues is in terms of actual experience. Some secondary principles of the natural law are discovered through experience (see S. T. II-II, 47, 15). Experience with life is one reason why the elderly should be consulted (see S. T. II-II, 49, 3). Since experience is always of and within a context, the sensitivity of each theorist to experience is, *a fortiori*, an openness to the importance of context for practical reasoning, moral choice, and action.

As noted earlier, their openness to the role of experience in shaping moral theory places them in what I have called the more "hands on" camp of ethical theorists. An example of this in Aquinas is his discussion of how the correct application of natural law principles depends on context (see S. T. II-II, 94, 4; also S. T. I-II, 100, 8). One specific example is the correct application of the principle that goods entrusted to another should be returned to their owner. Though this principle is legitimate, there are contexts in which it ought not to be followed, for example, when the restored goods would be used for fighting against one's country.[7] Sensitivity to context allows for exceptions to the applicability of principles. This indicates that principles can be reformulated with specifications that restrict their scope. Thus, Aquinas admits that principles of practical reason and natural law can be changed on the basis of experience to better fit specific contexts. Reinforcement for this conclusion is found in S.T. II-II, 94, 5, where Aquinas admits that natural law can be changed in various ways, though not so that the primary precepts of natural law cease to exist. Natural law can be added to, he says, since additions have been made for the benefit of human life. Presumably, reasoning from experience allows us to discover such benefits.

Aquinas's views on exactly which principles can be circumscribed by the exigencies of context are clarified in S. T. I-II, 100, 8, where he identifies the intention of the lawgiver as a norm for determining when dispensations or exceptions to principles are permissible. In some circumstances, following a principle, and thereby acting according to the letter of the law, would frustrate the intention of the lawgiver. In these cases, exceptions should be granted so that the intention of the lawgiver is preserved. Aquinas distinguishes precepts that contain the intention of the lawgiver from those that lack it. Some precepts, he claims, contain "…the very preservation of the common good, or the very order of justice and virtue…" (S. T. I-II, 100, 8). Because of this, they contain the intention of the lawgiver. Consequently, dispensations from these principles are not permitted. Examples of such precepts include laws, enacted in communities, that no one should work to destroy the commonwealth, that no one should betray the state to its enemies, and that no one should do injustice or evil. Principles subordinate to these that determine specific modes of procedure do admit of dispensation or exception, provided that the dispensations do not subvert the intention of the lawgiver.

Since some natural law principles (which are also principles of practical reason) are necessary and cannot be changed, one might think that

---

[7] Interestingly, the question of whether to restore goods to their rightful owner when they might be used against one's country is used to illustrate *gnome*, the virtue of discrimination in judgment associated with prudence—thereby highlighting the interconnections between natural law and prudence (see S. T. II-II, 51, 4).

Aquinas here parts ways with Held on the role of experience in shaping moral theory. Reshaping has definite limits. Would Held disagree? For her, not all experience is capable of shaping moral theory, but only the special category of moral experience. Even moral experience does not always or necessarily cause changes in moral beliefs. However, since Held does not definitively identify moral principles that are immune to revision, and adopts a coherentist model that encourages change, she seems open to the possibility that moral experience could cause all of someone's moral principles to be changed or abandoned. This is consistent with a general feminist avoidance of universal, necessary principles. But for Aquinas, the primary precepts of natural law and the goods they specify are fixed.

Held is open to roles for emotion in ethics, and is willing to give it a guiding, as opposed to only a subsidiary function relative to the formation and adoption of moral principles and beliefs. Emotions do not loom large in Aquinas's views on prudence. When they appear in his writing, he is generally not enthusiastic. He and Held agree that some emotions are harmful. For example, he attributes vices associated with imprudence to lust (see S. T. II-II, 53, 6). Solicitude, caution, and docility seem to have an affective dimension, but each plays only a supportive role in enabling us to reason well. Moreover, Aquinas spends far more time analyzing the cognitive components of prudence than its affective elements—an emphasis which suggests a lack of regard for roles emotion can take in good practical reasoning. Despite this, he does allow space for regulative or directive roles for inclination and appetite—phenomena resembling emotions insofar as they have an affective or desiring dimension. We have natural inclinations to pursue the ends of human life. Aquinas remarks that these inclinations are the natural law, and that the natural law is the rational creature's participation in the eternal law (see S. T. II-II, 91, 2). The word "inclination" indicates being oriented toward something, which in turn suggests an affective or desiring component. Consistently with what God ordains for us, we naturally want such goods as self-preservation, for example, and naturally abhor and avoid that which threatens it (see S. T. II-II, 94, 2). Our natural inclinations show us, along with natural reason, the goods to seek and the evils to avoid. Given this partnership of reason and inclination, it is not inconceivable that defective reason could misdirect our pursuit and avoidance and that our natural inclinations could function as correctives. If so, Aquinas can allow a regulative or directive role for the emotion-like phenomenon of inclination—one that functions to correct deficiencies in reasoning. Direct evidence for a regulative or directive role for appetite is given in this passage: "Consequently, it is requisite for prudence, which is right reason about things to be done, that man be well disposed with regard to his ends: and this depends on the rectitude of his appetite" (S. T. I-II, 57, 4). Right appetite directs us appropriately toward our ends, and thus, appropriately regulates prudence. In a discussion of whether prudence is in the cognitive or the appetitive faculty, Aquinas includes this revealing paragraph:

> As stated above (P. I. Q 82, A. 4) the will moves all the faculties to their acts. Now the first act of the appetitive faculty is love, as stated above (I-II, Q. 25, AA. 1, 2). Accordingly prudence is said to be love, not indeed, essentially, but in so far as love moves to the act of prudence. Wherefore Augustine goes on to say that *prudence is love discerning aright that which helps from that which hinders us in tending to God.* Now love is said to discern because it moves the reason to discern. (II-II, 47, reply obj. 1; italics his)

At the least, this passage suggests the importance of an intrinsic affective or emotive element in prudence.

Relationship and collaboration are two further points of comparison and contrast. Aquinas is silent on the general topic of relationship, and does not mention women's relationships, such as mothering, which Held sees as fruitful for moral inquiry. In considering domestic prudence, he writes: "The father has in his household an authority like that of a king…" (S. T. 50, 3, reply obj. 3). This is a stark reminder that, despite commonalities, there are deep and serious differences between feminism and natural law theory, at least as found in Aquinas.

Despite this, there is precedent in Aquinas for preferring relationships to principles in cases of conflict. Consider again the principle that goods entrusted to another should be restored to their rightful owner. The principle as stated is justifiably overridden if the goods would be used against one's country. Why should one's country be that important? One views one's country as a good if one stands in a particular relationship to it— the relationship of being a loyal citizen. At stake in withholding the other's goods and thereby ostensibly acting contrary to principle is not only the abstract good of one's country, but that good as understood by someone who stands in a particular relationship to her country. If the principle can be overridden in these circumstances, it can also be overridden when it is likely that the restored goods would be used against one's parent or spouse. One justifiably overrides principle to protect these people, not just because doing so preserves the good of life or the good of family, but also because of the importance of the particular relationship in which one stands to the individual person who would be threatened. One's relationship is one of the factors that justify acting contrary to principle.

Reflecting on this example illustrates how thoroughly experiential Aquinas's natural law theory is. The primary precepts of natural law—self-preservation, sexual intercourse and care of offspring, knowing the truth about God, and living in society (see S. T. II-II, 94, 2)—articulate goods that are experienced in and through the individual lives we lead and the particular relationships we have. Herein lies a possible difference between Aquinas and Held on the value of relationships, however. For Held, relationships are valuable for their own sakes. It is not clear that the same is true for Aquinas. Rather, relationships are valuable because of the goods they instantiate.

Finding common ground on collaboration is easier, though here, too, differences emerge. Held writes approvingly of dialogic uses of reasoning that invite participation in moral discourse from a diversity of perspectives. Aquinas acknowledges the need for collaboration on moral questions in his discussion of counsel. Counsel is the first act of prudence, and is essential for inquiry and deliberation. He acknowledges the propriety of seeking counsel not only about our own actions, but also about the actions of others close to us, for example, about the actions of a friend or a servant (see S. T. I-II, 14, 3, reply obj. 4). Is Aquinas as open as Held to the need for a diversity of perspectives? It seems not, for he advises those seeking counsel to consult "...old folk who have acquired a sane understanding of the ends in practical matters" (S. T. II-II, 49, 3). Had he been genuinely interested in a diversity of perspectives, he would have advised seeking a wider range of consultants.

One final observation. Aquinas's sensitivity to experience, context, and collaboration suggests that he, like Held, eschews such devices for ethical reasoning as an impartial perspective or the ideal observer. Though the general principles of natural law are universal and necessary, they are applied in particular situations by concrete individuals. They are also shaped and made more determinate by the demands of experience. To my knowledge, nowhere does Aquinas state that the application and reshaping of these principles, or the use of prudence in the choice of means to ends, require individuals to shed their personal points of view and assume an impartial or ideal perspective. Aquinas's elaboration of the quasi-integral parts of prudence indicates that, for him, reasoning about the means to the ends of human life is very much rooted in the "here and now" and performed by all-too-imperfect persons. Precisely because of the situatedness and finitude of the persons who reason, care must be taken to be aware of all circumstances and future contingencies. Reasoning well in ethical matters does not require abstracting from particulars, but getting the particulars right. With this, I believe, Held would agree.

IRRECONCILABLE DIFFERENCES?

A comparative study of Held and Aquinas reveals similarities as well as differences in their approaches to practical reason. Can we conclude anything instructive from this?

I believe we can. A first question is why we find these similarities and differences. One reason for the differences is that prudence for Aquinas is restricted to questions of means, whereas feminist moral inquiry for Held is amenable to the revision of existing ends and the discovery of new ones. This difference is significant. One of the aims of clarifying feminist methodology is to allow a robust substantive tradition in feminist ethics to emerge. The framework of that tradition has yet to be fully developed. It is unfinished business. Held's use of coherentism with its structural fluidity and openness to change is amenable to the construction of feminist frameworks. If there is any belief that is immune to revision in feminism, it is the belief in the importance for feminist theorizing of women's experiences, issues, and perspectives. By contrast, consider why prudence is, and can only be, about means. For Aquinas, the ends of human life are fixed and God-given through the natural law. Though there is a role for reason in adding to and enhancing these ends, they are, in the main, necessary. In the work of Aquinas, the framework of the natural law tradition is set by God's law. It is largely finished business. As with the rest of Aquinas's philosophy, this framing structure is part of a larger theology and theological commitments. Neither the general framework of natural law ethics nor the theological tradition that houses it can be abandoned or changed in essential respects.[8]

All of this has to do with what I regard as the "macro" level of ethical theory—the framing structures, the "big picture." Aquinas's framing structure is foundationalist and deductive. God is responsible for natural law, and the precepts of the natural law are ordered deductively from general to specific (see S. T. II-II, 91, 2; 94, 2). Held's framing structure is coherentist. At the "micro" level of ethical theory—in the trenches, where theory meets practice—the rigidity of Aquinas's deductivist model gives way. As Aquinas recognizes, despite the universal and necessary character of the general principles of natural law, they admit of qualifications and exceptions as one seeks to fit these abstract principles to particular experiences (see S. T. II-II, 94, 4). At the "micro" level—the level of experience, practicality, and imperfection—he is forced to admit the pragmatic truth of many of Held's observations. Experience can change theory; principles must be amended to give practical guidance. We cannot always decide which choices to make on our own; we must collaborate with others. Sometimes our reasoning fails; then, it is better to be guided by emotion. What he does not explicitly come around to is the view that preserving relationships for their own sake can be more important than perpetuating principles.

Are the differences in outlook irreconcilable? Aquinas's theory cannot be changed. At best, we are entitled to conclude that similarities exist between his theory of prudence and Held's feminist moral inquiry at the "micro" level where theory meets practice. At the "macro" level of theoretical frameworks, the differences are deep, pervasive, and apparently irreconcilable.

One such deep and irreconcilable difference merits special mention. Aquinas adopts many of Aristotle's assumptions about the natural inferi-

---

[8] I have left Aquinas's theological commitments aside in order to focus more directly on his philosophical uses of practical reason.

ority of women to men.[9] For example, in his commentary on Aristotle's *Politics*, Aquinas follows Aristotle in maintaining that women's reasoning powers are naturally weak and impeded by the force of emotion.[10] As a consequence, it would be difficult for women to achieve the constancy needed for intellectual virtue (see *Ibid.*). Aquinas links women's subordination to men to men's superior powers of rational discernment (see S. T. I, 92, 1; quoted in Allen, 400). He endorses Gorgias's view that different virtues apply to different groups of people and claims that silence is women's excellence, especially in the public order.[11] He quotes approvingly St. Paul's remarks that women who desire to learn should be taught by their husbands at home.[12] All of these views are anathema to feminists. Because Aquinas endorses them, his theory of natural law will never be compatible with feminism.

Must we therefore conclude that all natural law theories are incompatible with all feminist theories? That would be premature and overly pessimistic. Setting aside Aquinas's assumptions about women, which, one hopes, are not shared by contemporary natural law theorists, a benefit of the foregoing exercise is that it indicates how deep and meaningful convergence can be reached.

One way of progressing toward convergence at the "micro" level between feminism and contemporary natural law theory is to encourage work on areas of concern to both types of theory. Most contemporary natural law theorists who write about practical reason invoke Aquinas's views on practical reasoning. Unfortunately, some do not extensively develop in their own theories those views of Aquinas's that are similar to Held's, *viz.*, sensitivity to context in shaping practical principles; the collaborative dimension of practical reasoning; the value of emotion and its roles in practical reasoning; and the value of relationships. For example, though it is clear that practical reasoning is deeply connected with experience since it is reasoning about what to do, natural law theorists such as

[9] See the excellent discussion in Sister Prudence Allen, R. S. M., *The Concept of Woman: The Aristotelian Revolution*, 750 B. C. - A. D. 1250, 2d ed. (Grand Rapids, Michigan: William B. Eerdmans Publishing Company, 1997), pp. 385-407.

[10] See St. Thomas Aquinas, *In Octo Libris Policorum Aristotelis* (Quebec: Tremblay and Dion, 1940), Book I, p. 51; translated by Diane Gordon; quoted in Allen, p. 399.

[11] See Ibid.; quoted in Allen, p. 400.

[12] See Ibid.; quoted in Allen, p. 400.

Germain Grisez and John Finnis seem more concerned with deriving correct principles of practical reasonableness than with emphasizing the importance of context for forming these principles.[13] This is not to deny that Grisez and Finnis regard the principles of practical reason as *practical*.[14] It is simply to point out that the role of context in shaping principles and norms is not salient in their theories. Yet some in the natural law tradition, most notably Joseph M. Boyle, Jr., explicitly follow Aquinas in acknowledging that context can affect moral norms.[15] Moreover, to my knowledge, contemporary natural law theorists rarely recognize a collaborative dimension to practical reasoning, even though counsel is, for Aquinas, the first act of prudence. Here, too, there are promising exceptions. Boyle and Robert P. George realize that practical reasoning is located within communities and traditions.[16] Boyle explicitly recognizes a role for advisors in practical reasoning.[17] He and Finnis also acknowledge the value of emotion and roles for emotion in practical reasoning.[18] Emphasis on relationship finds its place in natural law theorizing in Finnis's recognition of friendship as a basic human good,[19] in comments on the value of

[13] See, for example, Germain Grisez, *The Way of the Lord Jesus*, Volume Three, *Difficult Moral Questions* (Quincy, Illinois: Franciscan Press, 1997), and John Finnis, *Natural Law and Natural Rights* (Oxford: Clarendon Press, 1980), chapter five.

[14] They stress this point in John Finnis and Germain Grisez, "The Basic Principles of Natural Law: A Reply to Ralph McInerny," *The American Journal of Jurisprudence* 26, pp. 22ff.

[15] See Joseph M. Boyle, Jr., "Moral Reasoning and Moral Judgment," *1984 Proceedings of the American Catholic Philosophical Association*, vol. LVIII (August 1985), pp. 39-40; see also Robert P. George, *In Defense of Natural Law* (Oxford: Clarendon Press, 1999), p. 255.

[16] See Joseph Boyle, "Natural Law and the Ethics of Traditions," in Robert P. George, ed. *Natural Law Theory: Contemporary Essays* (Oxford: Clarendon Press, 1992), pp. 12-13; and George, *In Defense of Natural Law*, p. 255.

[17] See Boyle, "Moral Reasoning and Moral Judgment," p. 48.

[18] See Boyle, "Ibid.," pp. 40ff; 46-48; John Finnis, *Aquinas* (New York: Oxford University Press, 1998), p. 119, note 81, where Finnis states that *prudentia* for Aquinas "... is not simply a matter of reason ... but is partly a matter of interest, desire, and disposition ..." and Finnis, *Fundamentals of Ethics* (Washington, D. C.: Georgetown University Press, 1983), p. 47, where he asserts that emotion of feeling is one aspect of the reality of human goods.

[19] See Finnis, *Natural Law and Natural Rights*, p. 88; pp. 141-44; *Fundamentals of Ethics*, pp. 144ff; on friendship in *Aquinas*, see Aquinas, p. 85.

marriage,[20] and in a general emphasis in natural law theory on the good of community.[21] Encouraging work on the foregoing topics could amplify and deepen existing points of contact between feminism and contemporary natural law theories.

Second, truly deep convergence can be reached by modifying the framing structures and assumptions of both feminism and natural law. Such revisions at the "macro" level are more fundamental and potentially far-reaching than changes of emphasis at the "micro" level. To achieve convergence in framing structures and assumptions, we needn't ask feminists to forego prioritizing women's issues, nor natural law theorists to relinquish their belief in God. Feminists can consider integrating God and natural inclinations into their theories, and can establish more fixed points of theory that are immune to coherentist revision. Natural law theorists can give a more prominent place to women's issues and perspectives, and entertain a more fluid conception of the ends of human life than is found in Aquinas. Some theorists will resist these changes. But some can, and have, begun to make accommodations. For example, some feminists have taken God and natural inclinations seriously. Some natural law theorists have taken women's issues to heart, and recognize the need to take gender concerns into account in conceptualizing human goods. Most of these people are theologians.[22] It is time for philosophers to follow suit.[23]

---

[20] See Finnis, *Aquinas*, pp. 143-54, for an interpretation of Aquinas's view; George, *In Defense of Natural Law*, chapter eight.

[21] For example, see Finnis, *Natural Law and Natural Rights*, chapter six; Finnis, *Aquinas*, chapters seven and eight; Boyle, "Natural Law and the Ethics of Traditions;" and Germain Grisez, Joseph Boyle, and John Finnis, "Practical Principles, Moral Truth, and Ultimate Ends," *The American Journal of Jurisprudence* 32, p. 138. [22] See note 1. For an example of a natural law theorist who takes gender issues into account, see Traina's discussion of Richard A. McCormick's views on sexuality and abortion in Traina, pp. 215-16.

[22] See note 1. For an example of a natural law theorist who takes gender issues into account, see Traina's discussion of Richard A. McCormick's views on sexuality and abortion in Traina, pp. 215-16.

[23] I am grateful to Lori Alward for inviting me to present an earlier version of this paper at a session of the International Natural Law Society, and to the audience at the session that met in conjunction with the American Catholic Philosophical Association on November 2, 2002 in Cincinnati, Ohio. I would also like to thank Lori for helpful suggestions, and Shelby Weitzel for her commentary.

DOES FEMINISM NEED NATURAL LAW
LIKE A FISH NEEDS A BICYCLE?
FEMINISM, AUTONOMY, AND THE HUMAN TELOS
Shelby Weitzel

INTRODUCTION

Does feminism need natural law? The answer will depend upon whom you ask. Most feminists will respond to the question with either a knee-jerk reaction that it most certainly does not, or puzzlement as to why one might think that it would. After all, it is no secret that natural law theory (or, at least, one prominent version of natural law theory) has been a keystone of the longstanding Western patriarchal tradition. This will be a, if not the, reason for a healthy skepticism among contemporary feminists. Not only are there historic ties between natural law theory and oppression, but natural law theory may also be too provincial for any feminist theory with global aspirations.

Nevertheless, there are women for whom natural law theory constitutes part of their philosophic and religious tradition. Some of these women have abandoned the tradition in the name of feminism but others think that natural law theory has something positive to offer. With this in mind, I would like to investigate Cristina Traina's argument that an updated Thomistic natural law theory has much to offer feminist theory. In making her case, Traina praises Martha Nussbaum's capabilities approach as providing some of what is lacking in feminist theory. However, Traina sees shortfalls in Nussbaum's view which appear to necessitate a further step towards natural law.

Two questions form the backbone of what follows. First, what is allegedly missing from feminist theory, and from Nussbaum's view in particular? Traina argues that feminist theory needs natural law because it alone can provide a "substantive telos." What Traina means by "substantive telos" will be extrapolated by contrasting her view with that of Martha Nussbaum—a view that is telic, but not substantive. Hence, although Nussbaum's view is admirable in many respects, it nevertheless falls short in a manner that can be repaired (uniquely) by Traina's version of natural law theory.

Second, is natural law able to provide what is missing without incurring too great a cost? If Traina were correct about the shortfalls of

Nussbaum's view, then this would suggest that feminists should incorporate natural law into their theory. This suggestion puts off other feminists such as Christina Pierce because, by her account, natural law theory is incompatible with autonomy. Hence, according to Pierce, whatever other problems there may or may not be with Nussbaum's view, it is preferable to the kind of natural law theory that Traina advocates. In this paper, I will argue that although natural law is not incompatible with autonomy in a way that should be of concern to feminists, an approach like Nussbaum's (whether one calls it natural law or not) nevertheless provides a better philosophical grounding for feminism than the type of natural law advocated by Traina.

WHY FEMINISM NEEDS NATURAL LAW

Traina believes that natural law theory needs feminism and that feminism needs natural law theory. Most feminists would agree with the former claim, but few would endorse the latter.[1] Why might one agree with Traina that feminism must adopt an overarching, substantive *telos* from a natural law perspective? To answer this question, consider the history of Western (liberal) feminism.

Western feminists have typically aimed at the elimination of injustice and inequality in the lives of women. Despite great success, feminists are far from completing their mission. Further work remains to be done within feminist theory itself and in the reform of society, and feminists disagree about what the next steps should be on both projects. What matters for the present investigation is that it has made sense to say that the conditions of women's lives can and ought to be improved. To make further progress, feminists must continue to advance meaningful claims about which states of affairs are better or worse for women.

In striving to eliminate injustice and inequality, feminists have tended to base their arguments on universal claims about the capacities and

---

[1] Even Traina encounters difficulty in arguing for the latter claim. Much of her book, *Feminist Ethics and Natural Law: The End of the Anathemas* (Washington, D.C.: Georgetown University Press, 1999), consists in showing that feminism and natural law theory employ similar methods and share many commitments to justice and human welfare. However, that feminism parallels natural law theory in many respects is insufficient to support her thesis.

dignity of women as human beings. These human capacities not only ground the claims about what is good for women (as humans), but also ground normative claims on women's status as persons. Western feminists have not needed to articulate a substantive human telos because the notion of a universal human nature grounded in reason and dignity was not considered controversial; what was considered controversial (and still is for some) is the extent to which women can exhibit human excellence. Many of the obstacles to women's achievements have been justified by incorrect empirical claims about what women are and can be, and much of the Western feminist tradition has consisted in disproving these incorrect claims.

According to Traina, Western feminism has now arrived at a crossroads. Postmodernists have undercut the normative grounding that has been so vital to pressing feminist claims in politics and ethics. Postmodernists have challenged the universal claims initially advanced by Enlightenment thinkers. In postmodernism, "Truth" represents a worldview that serves the interests of those who are powerful enough to shape social discourse. Although feminists in general have replaced allegedly "objective" claims about the nature of men and women with claims about gender socialization, postmodernists take these new claims one step farther; they deny that women constitute an identifiable group. There is no such thing as "woman," except as a social construction. Additionally, any "truths" about women's flourishing are taken to represent merely the view of some in a way that necessarily excludes the perspective and experience of others.

The postmodernist challenge threatens feminism in two ways. First, if women do not share a common "nature" or "condition," then on what grounds could women identify with one another? The lack of common ground generates a psychological problem of motivation, preventing the kind of unified front necessary to generate activism. Second, even if one can still create a solidarity that cuts across the myriad differences, postmodernist theory threatens one's ability to measure progress or to ground claims about how things ought to be made better. Feminists might still be able to press for changes, but their activism is cast as part of a struggle between the powerful and the marginalized, neither of which has a solid, moral grounding for their position.

Numerous philosophers have responded (in my opinion, successfully) to the postmodernist challenge, and so I will not consider it here.[2] Still, Traina is correct that feminist theory is at a crossroads. Multicultural feminists have amply demonstrated that whatever women have in common, we embrace different values and goals. Perhaps *the* challenge for contemporary feminism is striking that balance between extending and respecting the autonomy of women while maintaining a perspective which enables one to critically evaluate practices in which women engage.

In order to meet this challenge (and by extension, the postmodernist challenge), Traina claims that it is necessary to reintroduce universal claims about women and what is good for them. In her words, feminist ethics and politics "depends upon the possibility of making some authentically common claims rooted in commonly held visions of women's flourishing."[3] More specifically, solidarity requires strong, positive universal rights claims backed by anthropology: " a normative description of embodied human life."[4] Thus far, Traina's argument is not apt to disturb many non-postmodernist feminists. It is the next two claims that distinguish her.

According to Traina, not just any anthropology will do. Rather the anthropology has to be telic. By this she means that it must include ends for the individual and for society. Hence, what we ought to do is based at least somewhat on what we are "by nature." One does not have to look far to find controversy about what is or is not "natural," and many feminists resist relying on such claims at all.[5] But even if one did accept the argument thus far, one might take issue with Traina's final assumption,

---

[2] See for example, "What's Going On? Black Feminist Thought and the Politics of Postmodernism" in Patricia Hill Collins, *Fighting Words: Black Women & the Search for Justice* (Minneapolis: University of Minnesota Press, 1998), and Christine Pierce, *Immovable Laws, Irresistible Rights: Natural Law, Moral Rights, and Feminist Ethics* (Lawrence, Kansas: The University Press of Kansas, 2000).

[3] Traina, 6.

[4] Traina, 6.

[5] John Stuart Mill, for instance, argued persuasively that women ought to be given career and educational opportunities despite the fact that women's nature is unknown. A thin conception of the good is sufficient to support claims about what is good for women (as individual women). This approach leaves fairly open what women can, could, or should be. John Stuart Mill, *The Subjection of Women* (Indianapolis: Hackett Publishing Company, 1988), chapter 1.

which is that her version of natural law is uniquely suited to providing this much needed anthropology.

I say "her version" because there is an alternate view that relies upon a telic anthropology. One recent attempt to ground a feminist program with claims about human nature is Martha Nussbaum's capabilities approach. There are numerous ways in which we might attempt to measure human well-being: in terms of primary goods, welfare, functioning, or capabilities, to name a few. Nussbaum advocates measuring well-being in terms of capabilities for functioning. If we want to know if people are doing well, we can ask of them, "What are they able to do or to be?" Nussbaum offers a rough list of what is needed to support the human capabilities, which include adequate food, water and shelter, affiliation, play, and access to the environment. Once the capability for healthy relationships, meaningful work, and other vital components of a worthwhile life are accessible, it is then left up to each person to choose which capabilities to develop and exercise.[6] Traina admits that Nussbaum's approach offers a normative anthropology, that it is telic, and that it even goes so far as to include a thick, but vague conception of the good.[7]

Traina is generally supportive of Nussbaum's capabilities approach. Traina's objection is that Nussbaum's approach lacks "a substantive telos." Traina explains that because Nussbaum's capabilities theory leaves choice up to people regarding which capabilities to use and how, it fails to be sufficiently action guiding to constitute a constructive ethic.[8] Hence, her main worry is that Nussbaum does not go far enough. Although Traina does not say it, it appears that a sufficiently substantive telos would be detailed and organized enough to indicate the correct course of action rather than leave the choice up to the individual. Traina's account of natural law purports to provide feminist theory with that substantive telos.

---

[6] Martha Nussbaum, *Sex and Social Justice* (New York: Oxford University Press, 1999).

[7] Traina, 17.

[8] Traina, 315.

PIERCE'S CRITIQUE OF NATURAL LAW THEORY

Feminists have strongly objected to the telos that has historically been ascribed to women in natural law theory. Although there are many versions of natural law, according to Pierce, "the one consistent view seems to be that the specific reasons or purposes for things are inculcated in the essential nature of those things and that these reasons or purposes have a moral dimension."9 This has resulted in a longstanding condemnation of, among other practices, homosexuality, birth control, masturbation, and abortion. More recently proscriptions against the use of reproductive technologies and women in combat have been added to the mix. The view has effectively justified the oppression of homosexual and heterosexual women for centuries.

The feminist objections to traditional natural law theory are compelling, but may indicate the need to reform rather than abandon natural law theory. Perhaps the problem is not natural law, but the bigots who hide behind it. Just as Kantian feminists have argued that many of the misogynist conclusions drawn by Kant do not actually follow from Kant's theory, so too might feminists argue that a genuine natural law perspective would not warrant the historical admonitions. Looking to nature and to the wide variety of human viewpoints, a natural law position that does not already presume that what is natural is what favors the interests of (some) heterosexual men could yield conclusions that are neither sexist nor heterosexist.

The more philosophically interesting objection to natural law theory is Christine Pierce's claim that natural law is incompatible with autonomy. Assume for the moment that autonomy is an essential concept for any adequate feminist theory, and that natural law is incompatible with it. If this is the case, then any feminist should reject natural law theory regardless of what one believes the content of the natural law would be, for it is not enough to endorse a view that yields the correct conclusions; it must yield them for the right reasons. Now, whether or not natural law theory is incompatible with autonomy depends in part upon what one means by autonomy. And whether or not natural law is incompatible with feminism depends upon whether or not it is incompatible with a sense of autonomy

9 Pierce, 116.

that is in fact essential to feminism. What I will now argue is that there are three senses of autonomy, of which two are perfectly compatible with both natural law and feminism. While the third, more Kantian sense of autonomy is not compatible with natural law, neither is it essential for feminism. Hence, the claim that natural law theory is incompatible with autonomy is not in fact an objection that should trouble feminist natural law theorists.

Central to Pierce's notion of autonomy is the concept of the person.[10] In Kantian ethical theory, the reason why persons have dignity is because of our rationality. Our reason makes us capable of moral action and it is our reason that generates our duties to others and ourselves. Our reason also grounds the respect that others owe to us, where respect consists in recognizing our autonomy: our ability and our right to live according to our own reason. Furthermore, because of our autonomy, persons have a moral worth that distinguishes us from things. A person, unlike a thing, is not an object intended merely for the use of another. It follows that any view likening women to things fails to respect women's personhood, and by extension, autonomy. Such views are unacceptable from a feminist point of view. So if natural law likens women to things, then it too is unacceptable from a feminist point of view.

Pierce objects to natural law theory because it is incompatible with women's autonomy. In the course of drawing out her critique, it becomes clear that there are in fact three issues at stake—one pertaining to the role of choice, one pertaining to the moral worth of persons vis-à-vis each other, and one pertaining to the moral worth of persons as such. As we consider her objection, we can see that the three issues are linked, although as I will explain, they need not be.

According to Pierce, it is the views of Aristotle and Aquinas that have influenced the whole of Western civilization and thus constitute what we think of as traditional morality. Traditional morality dictates that different levels of being have different functions and that these functions are hierarchically ordered. Not only does each have a function, but also the function at each level is determined by the needs, interests, or good of beings at the next highest level. Whether the function of a person "determines"

---

10 Personhood is normative. It overlaps significantly with the biological category of humans, but there are humans that lack personhood and there are/may be persons that are not human.

or merely "shapes" or "narrows" her life choices depends on the amount of flexibility that is available in fulfilling one's function. A woman's telos has been limited to sexual, childrearing, and housekeeping services. These "proper" functions for women have also been deemed incompatible with the development of a woman's intellect, physical strength (for, say, sports or battle), or a sexuality that might be considered "her own."[11] For women, then, the telos has been construed rather restrictively.

In reaction to this sordid history of natural law, Pierce objects not only to the content of the traditional telos, but also to the very notion of a telos. She asserts that feminists should want to "stop short of providing such an end in order to 'leave room for a variety of ways of organizing goods and ends.'"[12] The implication is that natural law must always fail to leave room for a variety of ways of organizing goods and ends, at least for women. If Pierce is correct, then one problem with natural law theory is that it conflicts with women's autonomy by denying women the exercise of choice.

Furthermore, within natural law the hierarchy among persons has been explained by attributing moral superiority to some levels of being such that their purposes overrule the purposes of beings with lesser moral value.[13] As Pierce explains,

> A fundamental assumption of traditional natural law theory is that certain classes of persons are rightly treated as things, that is, their function or purpose is to serve the ends of someone else. For example... the function of women is defined in relation to others, not in relation to themselves. They have neither equality of authority nor autonomy....[14]

The problem is not merely that central components of women's lives involve husbands and children. Rather, the problem is the way in which women's lives have revolved around these relationships as though they were mere appendages to their husbands. Whatever fulfillment women

---

[11] For more detail, see Nancy Tuana, *Woman and the History of Philosophy* (St. Paul, MN: Paragon House, 1992) and Nancy Tuana, *The Less Noble Sex: Scientific, Religious, and Philosophical Conceptions of Woman's Nature* (Indianapolis: Indiana University Press, 1993).

[12] Pierce, 117.

[13] Pierce, 31.

[14] Pierce, 31.

might feel in carrying out their roles is irrelevant. The few options that women have had all pertain to serving others; any satisfaction that women might get from them is derivative. If Pierce is correct that natural law theory must regard women in this way, then natural law theory is incompatible with women's autonomy because it denies the moral worth of female persons vis-à-vis male persons.

Lastly, the hierarchy within which humans are subsumed below other beings generates further ramifications for human autonomy. To quote Pierce,

> ...Under natural law, persons are not recognized as the source of law. A person's natural end may be to serve the ends of others. Such a conclusion is incompatible with autonomy, for if I am autonomous, and if I am a source of law, I am not an object to be used by somebody else.[15]

To say the source of morality comes from within a person, because of her rationality, appears to be incompatible with the claim that there is a being superior to us. A child who is subject to a parent lacks this kind of autonomy, as does a servant to a master. Analogously, a human, within the system of natural law, is subordinate to the Supreme Creator. If Pierce is correct that according to natural law theory, the existence of a superior being implies that humans are to be treated as things, then natural law is incompatible with autonomy because it fails to properly value persons. This final issue also raises the eyebrows of many non-feminist ethicists, as the claim applies to men as well as to women. Feminists have been particularly vocal, however, because the consequences for women have been far more detrimental in application.

RESPONDING TO PIERCE: AUTONOMY AS EXERCISING CHOICE

If a person has no meaningful choices available to her, then regardless of what her capacities may be, she is unable to exercise her autonomy. When Pierce objects to the notion of a telos "in order to 'leave room

15 Pierce, 32.

for a variety of ways of organizing goods and ends,'"[16] the implication is that natural law fails to leave room for a variety of ways of organizing goods and ends. Furthermore, according to Pierce, "it is precisely by not telling women what purposes they ought to achieve that Nussbaum is able to assert that the capabilities view is compatible with autonomy and choice."[17] Within natural law theory, one does not get to choose one's purpose in life. But whether or not this means that one lacks autonomy remains to be seen.

The ambiguous conception of autonomy is not the only stumbling block in trying to arbitrate between Traina and Pierce. What it means to have a telos and what exactly follows from that further complicates matters. Depending upon what we take this to involve, we may find natural law to be either quite appealing or quite appalling.

First, consider what seems appealing. People who go about their daily lives as though nothing has meaning tend to feel empty or alienated. In natural law, humans have a purpose in the universe. We have both rights and responsibilities. We can make sense of our lives as going well or poorly. As stated, many would not find this objectionable. We want to believe that there is a reason why we exist, and we want to believe that our own existence matters.

But then we must ask, at what level does natural law assign purpose? Is it as a species? For instance, one might believe that as humans, our purpose involves being stewards of the earth. As such, the human purpose is general enough to encompass a wide variety of lifestyle choices. One might be a park ranger, an environmental lawyer, or one may make purchases reflecting care for the planet in terms of the clothes one wears, the form of transportation one uses, and the food one eats. At this level of description, however, the purposes are so general that ultimately they do not do much in the way of guiding the life choices of any particular individual. What it does succeed in doing is ruling out certain choices like poaching or polluting. It is worth noting, however, that this version of a telos would be unsatisfactory to Traina, as it would leave choice to the

[16] Pierce, 117.
[17] Pierce, 117-18.

individual, just as Nussbaum's view does. The substantive human telos must be more specific than this, but just to what extent is unclear.

What Pierce balks at is the idea that someone ought to fulfill a role that she doesn't want to fulfill. This has certainly been a problem for women. This may pose a problem for Traina's version of natural law theory because of her strict requirements for the human telos; for other versions of natural law, like Nussbaum's, it does not. In any case, we must be careful in distinguishing when it is proper to be obligated to do what one does not want to do. That some of the courses of action that we might like to choose are ruled out on moral grounds does not imply that one lacks autonomy. That there are some things that we are not supposed to do is a fact of morality (whether morality is understood in terms of natural law, Kantian ethics, or utilitarianism). Similarly, that there are things that we are supposed to do that we do not want to do is a fact of morality. So at times it is not morally problematic that someone is supposed to do something that she does not want to do. Suppose I am very good at neurosurgery, but I dislike it intensely. If there is a shortage of qualified neurosurgeons, and if the pursuit of neurosurgery is not done at the expense of other, more widely needed forms of health care, then perhaps I do have an obligation to pursue that career. And perhaps ultimately that is acceptable since neurosurgeons are respected and well-paid. What is repugnant is that others might force me to be a neurosurgeon (to the likely detriment of my patients). But I see no reason to believe that natural law theory entitles some to coerce others.

What is supposed to simplify matters somewhat in natural law is that a person will find satisfaction in fulfilling her function (She is flourishing, after all). If a person hates doing what she is "supposed" to do, then either there is something defective about that person, or what she is supposed to do has been misconstrued. Historically, women who have balked at their "destiny" have been labeled defective instead of taking the other path. This says more about the people who have applied natural law theory than it does about natural law theory. It seems plausible that the concern that Pierce has—that a woman will be justifiably forced to fulfill a [biological] destiny that is not her own—falls by the wayside once people apply natural law theory in a more responsive manner.

Even though some courses of action are forbidden and others are morally permissible or morally required, it is still the case that a great deal of choice is involved in pursuing the morally permissible and required ends. To illustrate, consider the following example. Many people, especially within the natural law tradition, have claimed that children are a worthwhile end to pursue. Let's assume that this is true. What does this mean for any particular woman? She has a number of choices. First, she may decide to remain childless and to avoid interaction with children; this is acceptable because raising children is one end available to her, not the only end. Alternatively, she may decide to remain childless, but play a role in the lives of children as an aunt, volunteer, pediatrician, or teacher. She may decide to conceive and bear children, or perhaps she may choose to adopt children. That any of these choices matter presumes that there are ends worth pursuing, some of which have to do with children, and some of which do not. Furthermore, some of the ends have to do with having a genetically related child while others do not.

From the fact that there is value in bearing, raising, adopting, or sharing lives with children, it does not follow that any particular person must do this. If it is important for the species to continue, then somebody must do this, but no one person, or gender, must. Given the physical, emotional and intellectual needs of children, all of which have a biological aspect, there are better and worse ways to care for children. Nature does, to some extent, demand that certain kinds of work be done; but it does not follow that any particular person must be the one to do it.[18] Should it turn out that no one wants to do the work, then we must distribute the work in a fair manner. So while there may be other conceptions of autonomy that are incompatible with a natural law perspective, the most obvious sense of having choices is not denied to a person within the natural law tradition.

AUTONOMY AS BEING AN END IN ONESELF

As Pierce explains, natural law has indicated that certain types of humans are designed to perform different functions. That people have different functions is not necessarily a problem; what matters is that traditionally the function of some has been to serve as a thing. Aristotle was happy to assign roles to slaves, children, and women tout court. At least two aspects of this are objectionable. 1) It assumes that these groups are

---

[18] See for example, Sarah Blaffer Hrdy, *Mother Nature: Maternal Instincts & the Shaping of the Species* (London: Vintage Books, 2000), and Eva Kittay, *Love's Labor: Essays on Women, Equality, and Dependency* (New York: Routledge, 1999).

so homogeneous that such generalizations are accurate. 2) It assumes that some groups of humans are legitimately subordinated to other groups of humans; their function is not the good of a whole in which everyone is valued equally, but rather, their function is to serve the good of the dominant (i.e. male, property-owning) class.

Regarding 1), the overgeneralizations of the traditional natural law system are not essential to natural law theory as such. We can remove them while leaving in place the notion that certain types of people are best suited to fulfill certain kinds of roles. Plato's *Republic* serves as one example of an argument concerning function that does not assume all women have the same function. The idea that we all have different roles to play in life appeals to many people. Many of us seek our niche—that job or set of relationships that contributes to the good of society, which we are good at, and which gives us pleasure. This is what it means to find our calling in life.

Some of the concerns raised by the neurosurgeon example reemerge here. In seeking our calling in life, we find ourselves in situations not of our making. For example, as family members age or fall ill, they need care. Some of us do not want to spend our time and effort as caregivers, but if we fail to provide it (directly or by hiring someone else to perform the services) then we have failed to be decent people. It is understandable why one would react negatively to the claim that what one ought to do is independent of what one wills. Visions of oppressive, totalitarian disutopias come to mind. But there is nothing about natural law that entitles some to subjugate others.

Additionally, it is not difficult to envision a version of natural law that denies 2). John Locke, for instance, claimed that it is not possible for people to be born slaves. Much of the concern about autonomy pertains to one version of the view, but does not appear to be essential to natural law theory as such.

AUTONOMY AS THE SOURCE OF LAW

The third aspect of the autonomy objection has to do with humanity's place in the grand scheme of things. Even if all humans are moral equals, they are still subject to a design not of their making. The question is, "Is this a problem for feminists?" Pierce argues that it is. Recall her claim that,

...under natural law, persons are not recognized as the source of law. A person's natural end may be to serve the ends of others. Such a conclusion is incompatible with autonomy, for if I am autonomous, and if I am a source of law, I am not an object to be used by somebody else.[19]

Pierce connects the source of moral law with the status of humans as persons. More specifically, within her view, if a human is not the source of the moral law, then that human is not a person, and therefore is a thing. This problem is compounded by the traditional view of humans as subservient to God. Within the historic worldview, because humans exist "below" God, our function is to serve the interests of God and our good is "overruled" by His.

Pierce's concern is only a problem for feminists if feminism must rely on a particular conception of personhood in which persons are the source of the moral law. Being the source of the law has to do with the origin of the law, of "where it comes from." But does the source of the moral law have to come from women (and men) to be feminist? I think the answer is "no." What has been a problem is that some humans, in seeking their self-interest, abuse and exploit other humans. Material resources, opportunities for work and education, and respect for bodily integrity and self-determination have not and are not distributed in a just manner. The injustice and inequality that feminists target pertains to humans vis-à-vis other humans. The proper locus of concern, then, is with the content of the moral law.

To achieve the goal of justice, one does not need to rely on a view of humans as the source of moral law. Pierce is correct that if I am a source of law, then I am not an object to be used by somebody else. It does not follow that if I am not the source of moral law, that I am therefore an object to be used by others. In natural law theory, we participate in the natural law because of our reason. We do not construct morality, but we do construct our understanding of what morality demands through the exercise of practical reason. We do our best to understand what the right and the good are. This is enough to distinguish us as persons; this is enough to ground our right to exercise our autonomy.

[19] Pierce, 32.

Recall that for Pierce, if there is a being with superior intellect and power then it follows that humans are to be considered as things. It is not clear why this has to be the case. There is a growing body of evidence indicating that dolphins exhibit rationality; let us assume for the moment that they do. If so, then dolphins are moral beings. Whether they are more or less rational than we are, they deserve respect. Although they differ from us, we ought not to use them for our own purposes. Similarly, it does not matter how powerful or knowledgeable other beings are; humans have surpassed the threshold of rationality that makes us autonomous. Just as we have duties towards other persons without thereby becoming like things with respect to those other persons, so too might we have duties to God without thereby becoming a thing with respect to God.

Part of the problem may be a misunderstanding of what it means "to serve." To serve is to attend, to promote and to render assistance. It is to take up a burden or responsibility in the name of something or someone other than oneself. Some forms of service are morally problematic and others are morally exemplary. The moral worth of one's service may be determined by the end one serves or the way in which one serves. If one is exploited in the performance of a service, then one is treated as a thing. But there are other, nonexploitative ways to be of service. To serve one's country or God is not necessarily to be treated as a mere thing; it is, for many people, precisely the way in which we express our humanity.

CONCLUSION

Several lessons can be learned from this simple attempt to define the parameters of a debate between the feminists that are inclined to adopt a natural law perspective and those who are inclined to reject it. Some of these lessons have to do with natural law, some with feminism, and some with their intersection.

First, an important distinction must be maintained between one historically relevant version of natural law and natural law theory as such. There is a world of difference between what natural law has been and what it can be. It is common to conflate the two, but any feminist with philosophical tendencies should be able to maintain the distinction. Most of the feminist criticisms, including those of Christine Pierce, are legitimately leveled at the mainstream, dominant version of natural law theory. This leaves open whether or not there is a natural law theory that can avoid these objections—one that could be relevant if not beneficial to feminism.

At first glance, Martha Nussbaum's capabilities approach appears to be just such a view. While it does not "claim to read facts of 'human nature' from biological observation,"[20] as the historically relevant version of natural law has done, "it takes biology into account as a relatively constant element of human experience."[21] These elements, combined with circumstances known to people worldwide—hunger, disease, aging, and competition—constitute "the human condition." The results of the interaction vary widely according to culture and geography, but basic universal truths continue to underlie the differences. There are conditions that must be met in order for any human being's life to be truly human; the capabilities approach delineates these conditions.

Second, whether or not feminism "needs" natural law also depends on what feminism is and can be. Fortunately, feminist theorists have learned to be open to self-evaluation in this way, because they are acutely aware of what can happen when one fails to exercise vigilance against a dominant viewpoint (even when that viewpoint is itself feminist). As Traina notes, feminists should consider what to aim for as they dismantle oppression. If feminists want to do more than give a negative account (emphasizing what has been wrong and eliminating it), then they must offer at least the outlines of a positive account to take the place of the status quo.

According to Traina, in order to provide an adequate positive account, it is necessary to have some sort of substantive telos as part of one's ethical theory. She believes that even Nussbaum's view is inadequate for this task, although why is difficult to discern. On the one hand, Traina draws heavily from Nussbaum's work and openly supports it:

> Among natural law's most important reminders to feminist ethics is that a "thick, vague" description of goods *is* vague: it accommodates and even anticipates a telic anthropology but— in Nussbaum's case, intentionally—provides no telos. *This is as it should be* [emphasis mine]. Feminism as I have present-

20 Nussbaum, 40.
21 Nussbaum, 40.

ed it is a coherent set of critical and constructive tools, not a comprehensive moral theory; and a feminist political in a society governed by Enlightenment liberal assumptions must leave room for a variety of ways of organizing goods and ends.[22]

On the other hand, Traina must believe that Nussbaum's view falls short, for she continues by adding:

> But if concrete, everyday moral reason is practical reason it must be able to organize its ends; therefore it needs to adopt a thick telic anthropology and with it guidelines for organizing and choosing among goods.[23]

Moreover,

> The transition from the critical to the constructive stance depends upon recognizing that even a feminist politics like Martha Nussbaum's expresses the end formally rather than substantively: the provision of all that women would need in order to cross the threshold of integral flourishing if they chose to do so. Certainly Nussbaum's list of conditions for free choice contains elements that no feminist ethic can do without...Yet this vision is neither concrete enough to guide an individual's daily moral life nor compelling enough to transform the elements of the threshold from mere options to goods worth pursuing.[24]

In Nussbaum's defense, one might simply disagree with Traina that there is a need for a "positive" or "constructive" feminist ethic. Even if Traina is right about the need for a constructive feminist ethic, it does not follow that Nussbaum's view is incorrect. It may just be incomplete, and Nussbaum herself has admitted as much. Her view is meant to be a partial theory of justice. As she sees it, it is both important and feasible to significantly erode current sources of oppression, without having to develop a substantive theory of the good. I am inclined to agree with her. Feminism seems to be doing just fine without a thoroughly articulated

---

[22] Traina, 158.

[23] Traina, 158.

[24] Traina, 315.

substantive telos. The gains of feminism have greatly improved the lives of women all over the world and will continue to do so.

Even if we accept the need for a constructive ethic, it is not clear that feminism requires a substantive telos in order to yield constructive ethics for women. In Nussbaum's field work, the Indian women who have won the right to work and formed their own collectives do not report that they have merely been freed from oppression; they describe the ways in which their lives are now better, if not all they hoped for. It is not as though they are fish out of water, with no sense of place, or with no idea of how to proceed.

The concerns that Traina expresses about the choices facing women (and all humans, actually) are difficult to discern. By emphasizing that a substantive telos is detailed and comprehensive enough to guide the daily lives of humans, Traina appears to limit the role of choice in an individual's life far more than any liberal thinker would tolerate. Even if Pierce is right about Traina in this respect, what this indicates is that a version of natural law like Nussbaum's is preferable, not that we must reject all versions of natural law.

However, Traina's objection to Nussbaum is not about the role of, or need for, choice, but rather about the source of the value of our endeavors. The mere fact of having choice about what capabilities one can develop is not what makes the capabilities good. Mere choice is not sufficient to result in a good life. Rather, choices become meaningful because the content of the choices is meaningful, and the telos is where the meaningfulness originates. Traina's mistake is in thinking that Nussbaum does not see this. In compiling the list of human capabilities, Nussbaum does articulate the human telos sufficiently to indicate what kinds of endeavors are worth pursuing. For example, if work were not meaningful in its own right or as a means to other endeavors worth pursuing, it would not have made it on the list of human capabilities.

So if there is a problem with Nussbaum's view, it cannot be that Nussbaum's view offers no guidelines for what contributes to a meaningful life. Rather, it must have to do with the fact that an overarching telos ensures that goods and ends *cohere* sufficiently to constitute a "good life" and not merely form a set of discrete, unrelated goods and ends. If one is left free to develop one's capacities, but does so with no rhyme or reason, then something has gone wrong.

If we leave choices up to individuals, it is true that some people run the risk of having an unbalanced life. Beginning with John Stuart Mill, liberals have explained why we must run this risk if we are to respect human individuality and autonomy. Having been adequately addressed elsewhere, this risk is clearly a necessary evil in a free society, and so does not really pose a problem for Nussbaum's view, any more than it does for any other liberal political theory. Besides, while the ten human capacities listed by Nussbaum are discrete, it is not as though policy will facilitate one capacity in a vacuum. In designing ways to facilitate education for women, for example, a just policy will enable women to pursue education compatibly with raising children, or at least provide women with the power to refrain from having children while pursuing their education. In this way, goods do cohere even though no overarching judgment has been made about who must do what and in what order.

In short, Traina is mistaken that feminism needs a telos that is more substantive than Nussbaum's. This is good news. As Traina must know, it is currently fashionable abroad to reject anything that smacks of Western imperialism. Part of what motivates Nussbaum's approach is the fact that,

> We can hardly be charged with imposing a foreign set of values upon individuals or groups if what we are doing is providing support for basic capacities and opportunities that are involved in the selection of any flourishing life and then leaving people to choose for themselves how they will pursue flourishing. Any universalism that has a chance to be persuasive in the modern world, must... be a form of political liberalism.[25]

There are pragmatic concerns that feminists must take into account, and Nussbaum's view is better able to navigate them.

More importantly from a philosophical perspective, Nussbaum's view is superior because it carves out an important place for the role of choice in a flourishing life. Traina portrays all liberals as valuing the maximization of choice as good in itself.[26] This is as unfair to liberal theory as the portrayal of all natural law theorists as homophobic, misogynist

[25] Nussbaum, 9.

[26] Traina, 27.

Neanderthals is to natural law. Humans are not like plants; if, as adults, we remain passive as someone else provides us with food, water and the like, then we are not living a fully human life. This is why practical reason itself figures prominently in Nussbaum's list of human capabilities. What it is to be fully human involves the exercise of reason. In order to develop and express ourselves as mature persons we must reflect and make choices, even if at times the choices we make are less than ideal. This does not undercut or threaten in any way the achievement of the human telos, as the well-reasoned, disciplined exercise of choice is itself part of human excellence.

ANNOTATED BIBLIOGRAPHY[1]

Works especially illustrative of the focus of this issue—feminism and natural law—are emphasized below

ALCOFF, Linda Martin, "Is the Feminist Critique of Reason Rational?," *Philosophic Exchange: Annual Proceedings*. 1995-96; 26: 59-79.

[Some philosophers have expressed the concern that the feminist critique of reason may undermine the primary strategy women have at our disposal to invalidate sexist beliefs, i.e., reason. Both Martha Nussbaum and Sabina Lovibond are concerned about feminist philosophy's relationship to philosophy, both question whether feminism rightly criticizes the canon as fundamentally patriarchal, and they also wonder whether feminism can coherently critique philosophical methodology given that it must use that same methodology in its critique. In this paper, I try to allay these legitimate concerns by linking that feminist critique of reason with the ongoing critique of reason within philosophy since Kant.]

ANTONY, Louise M., and WITT, Charlotte, eds., *A Mind of One's Own* (Boulder: Westview Press, 1993).

ANTONY, Louise M., "Natures and Norms," *Ethics: An International Journal of Social, Political, and Legal Philosophy*. October 2000; 111(1): 8-36.

ARNESON, Richard J., "Perfectionism and Politics," *Ethics: An International Journal of Social, Political, and Legal Philosophy*. October 2000; 111(1): 37-63.

CAHILL, Lisa Sowle, *Between the Sexes: Foundations for a Christian Ethics of Sexuality* (Fortress Press, 1985).

---

[1] Most of the abstracts are based on or are replications of the authors' or publishers' abstracts, which are printed in the online version of the *Philosopher's Index*.

CAHILL, Lisa Sowle, *Sex, Gender and Christian Ethics* (New York: Cambridge University Press, 1996).

CAHILL, Lisa Sowle, "Sex, Marriage, and Community in Christian Ethics," *Thought: Fordham University Quarterly.* March 1983; 58: 72-81.

[This article elucidates Christianity's distinctive framework for assessing sexuality. In the New Testament, morality is not itself a focus, but is discussed only in relation to communal life. Writing from different historical perspectives, Saint Paul advises celibacy, and Aquinas calls marriage a "sacrament." Despite differences, both are concerned primarily with the ways celibacy, marriage, and sexual activity enhance or destroy the faith community, rather than with either individual fulfillment or isolated acts.]

CAHILL, Lisa Sowle, "Toward a Christian Theory of Human Rights," *Journal of Religious Ethics.* Fall 1980; 8: 277-301.

CAHILL, Lisa Sowle, "Women, Marriage, Parenthood: What Are Their Natures?," *Logos: Philosophic Issues in Christian Perspective.* 1998; 9: 11-35.

CARD, Claudia, ed., *Feminist Ethics* (Lawrence: University Press of Kansas, 1991).

[This book includes contributions by Maria Lugones, Joyce Trebilcot, Marilyn Frye, Christine Pierce, Alison Jaggar, Bat-Ami Bar On, Ruth Ginzberg, Lynne McFall, Marilyn Friedman, Victoria Davion, Michele Moody-Adams, Elizabeth Spelman, Annette Baier, Sarah Hoagland, and Claudia Card. Topics include cultural pluralism, postmodernism, terrorism, survival ethics, bitterness, integrity, partiality, trust, and care ethics.]

CARD, Claudia, "Stoicism, Evil, and the Possibility of Morality," *Metaphilosophy.* October 1998; 29(4): 245-253.

[Martha Nussbaum's work has been characterized by a sustained critique of Stoic ethics, insofar as that ethics denies the validity and importance of our valuing things that elude our control. This essay explores the idea that the very possibility of morality, understood as social or interpersonal ethics, presupposes that we do value such things. If my argument is right, Stoic ethics is unable to recognize the validity of morality (so understood) but can at most acknowledge duties to oneself. A further implication is that moral luck, so far from undermining morality as some have held, is presupposed by the very possibility of morality.]

CHARLESWORTH, Hilary, "Martha Nussbaum's Feminist Internationalism," *Ethics: An International Journal of Social, Political, and Legal Philosophy*. October 2000; 111(1): 64-78.

CROCKER, David A., "Functioning and Capability: The foundations of Sen's and Nussbaum's Development Ethic," *Political Theory: An International Journal of Political Philosophy*. November 1992; 20(4): 584-612.

CURRAN, Angela, "Form as Norm: Aristotelian Essentialism As Ideology (Critique)," *Apeiron: A Journal for Ancient Philosophy and Science*. December 2000; 33(4): 327-364.

[The author examines the criticisms of Aristotelian essentialism (AE) recently presented by Richard Rorty and feminist philosopher Elizabeth Spelman, as well as looking at Martha Nussbaum's defense of AE as a tool for political critique. She argues that both those who condemn Aristotelian essentialism as ideologically suspect, and those, like Nussbaum, who find Aristotle valuable for current political theorizing misinterpret him in important ways. In doing so, these authors miss an opportunity to understand the possibilities and potential uses of AE in relation to contemporary political theorizing, as well as the problems with Aristotle's own misappropriation of his essentialism.]

CURRAN, Charles E., FARLEY, Margaret A., and MCCORMICK, S. J., Richard A., eds., *Feminist Ethics and the Catholic Moral Tradition.* (New York/Mahwah, New Jersey: Paulist Press, 1996).

DEVEAUX, Monique, "Political Morality and Culture: What Difference Do Differences Make?," *Social Theory and Practice: An International and Interdisciplinary Journal of Social Philosophy.* July 2002; 28(3): 503-518.

ESTLUND, David M., and NUSSBAUM, Martha C., eds., *Sex, Preference, and Family: Essays on Law and Nature* (New York: Oxford University Press, 1997).

[The public furor over issues of same-sex marriages, gay rights, pornography and single-parent families has erupted with a passion not seen since the 1960s. It is a battle being fought, in large part, over where to draw the line between law and nature, between the political and the personal, the social and the biological. It is an important struggle to resolve, for as we move into the next century our culture is redefining itself in fundamental ways. How we decide these questions will determine much about the kind of society we and our children will live in. Contributors to this volume include Michele Moody-Adams, Martha Nussbaum, Susan Moller Okin, Nancy Rosenblum, Stephen Macedo, Catharine MacKinnon, David Estlund, Richard Posner, Janet Halley, Cass Sunstein, Paul Weithman, Martha Minow, William Eskridge, Jr., William Galston, and Sara McLanahan.]

FREEBERG, Ellen, *Regarding Equality: Rethinking Contemporary Theories of Citizenship, Freedom, and the Limits of Moral Pluralism* (New York: Lexington Books, 2002).

[The book offers an analysis of the relationship between equality and pluralism. Tackling an issue central to modern political thought, Freeburg highlights the struggle to characterize citizens as equals while respecting their moral, religious, and cultural diversity. The work ably contrasts and critiques the prevailing model for balancing equality with pluralism from thinkers Amartya Sen, Martha Nussbaum, John Rawls, Amy Gutmann, Dennis Thompson, Michael Oakeshott, and Drucilla Cornell. From these liberal, democratic, and conservative approaches to equality and pluralism, Freeburg builds a theory of responsive regard: reciprocal civility between citizens that forms a chastened conception of what we share as free and equal citizens.]

FREUND, Ernst, and NUSSBAUM, Martha, *The Feminist Critique of Liberalism* (Lawrence: University of Kansas, 1997).

GAARD, Greta, ed., *Ecofeminism: Women, Animals, and Nature* (Philadelphia: Temple University Press, 1993).
[This volume includes contributions by Greta Gaard, Janis Birkeland, Lori Gruen, Stephanie Lahar, Linda Vance, Ellen O'Loughlin, Josephine Donovan, Carol J. Adams, Chaia Heller, Marti Kheel, and Huey-li Li.]

GAHL, Jr., Robert A., "From the Virtue of a Fragile Good to a Narrative Account of Natural Law," *International Philosophical Quarterly*. December, 1997; 37(4): 457-472.
[After describing claims against the compatibility of virtue and natural law theories, I draw from Pamela Hall's "Narrative and Natural Law" to argue for a reading of Aquinas capable of reconciling virtues and natural law. Martha Nussbaum's insightful virtue theory fails to explain moral experience insofar as it emphasizes the tragic character of life. The narrative moral epistemology embedded in Aquinas's thought shows the interdependency of law and virtues. A narrative account of natural law can be used to overcome tragic complexity and to tell a rationally defensible, comic story about the moral agent's ecstatic quest for the transcendent.]

GALSTON, William A., "Democracy and Value Pluralism," *Social Philosophy and Policy*. Winter 2000; 17(1): 255-268.

GLOVER, Jonathan, and NUSSBAUM, Martha, eds., *Women, Culture, and Development: A Study of Human Capabilities* (New York: Clarendon-Oxford Press, 1995.)

HOLLINGER, David A., "Not Universalist, Not Pluralists: The New Cosmopolitans Find Their Own Way," *Constellations: An International Journal of Critical and Democratic Theory*. June 2001; 8(2): 236-248.

[The new cosmopolitanism had emerged in the last several years as a distinctive theoretical outlook best understood if sharply distinguished from both the universalism of which Martha Nussbaum is a prominent representative and the pluralism for which Will Kymlicka has become the most widely discussed advocate. Since the deficiencies of Nussbaum's universalism have been widely noted, it is more important now to make theorists aware of the narrowness of Kymlicka's position.]

HRDY, Sarah Blaffer, *Mother Nature: A History of Mothers, Infants, and Natural Selection* (New York: Pantheon Books, 1999).

HRDY, Sarah Blaffer, "Raising Darwin's Consciousness: Females and Evolutionary Theory," *Zygon: Journal of Religion and Science*. June 1990; 25(2): 129-137.

[Early studies of primate social behavior were distorted by observational, methodological, and ideological biases that caused researchers to overlook active roles played by females in the social lives of monkeys. Primatology provides a particularly well-documented case illustrating why research programs in the social and natural sciences need multiple studies that enlist researchers from diverse backgrounds.]

KACZOR, Christopher, "Exceptionless Norms in Aristotle?: Thomas Aquinas and Twentieth-Century Interpreters of the 'Nicomachean Ethics'," *Thomist: A Speculative Quarterly Review*. January 1997; 61(1): 33-62.

[Within the context of larger debates in Thomistic ethics, the author presents the arguments of Martha Nussbaum, Nancy Sherman and W. F. R. Hardie that either explicitly or implicitly undermine the possibility of exceptionless norms in Aristotle's *Nicomachean Ethics*. Next, Thomas Aquinas's reading of the *Nicomachean Ethics* in his *Sententia libri ethicorum* is contrasted with these modern interpreters of Aristotle. The very analogies used by Aristotle suggest a place for exceptionless norms as does the explicit teaching of *Nicomachean Ethics* II, 6. Some possible responses to Nussbaum, Sherman and Hardie are presented in the final section.]

KITTAY, Eva Feder, *Love's Labor: Essays on Women, Equality, and Dependency* (New York: Routledge, 1999).

KITTAY, Eva Feder, and MEYERS, Diana, eds., *Women and Moral Theory* (Totowa: Rowman-Littlefield, 1987).

[This volume includes contributions by Carol Gilligan, Annette Baier, Michael Stocker, Christina Hoff Sommers, Kathryn Pyne Addelson, Virginia Held, Thomas E. Hill, Jr., Diana Meyers, Seyla Benhabib, George Sher, Marilyn Friedman, Jonathan Adler, Sara Ruddick, Mary Fainsod Katzenstein, David Laitin, Lizbeth Hasse, and Sandra Harding.]

MAHADEVAN, Kanchana, "Capabilities and Universality in Feminist Politics," *Journal of Indian Council of Philosophical Research*. 2001; 18(4): 75-105.

[This paper interrogates Martha Nussbaum's universal conception of human capabilities or "goods" from the gendered perspective of so-called developing countries such as India. It argues that despite being nonmetaphysical, her position is not entirely successful in addressing gender disparity in India. For Nussbaum's substantial list of capabilities is implicitly rooted in Western liberalism and also encourages paternalism. The paper finally argues that given its formalism, Jurgen Habermas's proceduralism is more suitable to feminist concerns in the pluralistic Indian context. But one would have to move beyond

Habermas, considering that he treats dialogue as given in the life-
world.]

MCKERLIE, Dennis, "Aristotle's Theory of Justice," *Southern Journal
of Philosophy*. Spring 2001; 39(1): 119-141.

[This paper contends that the heart of Aristotle's theory of justice is
the desert-based principle of proportional equality schematically
described in the *Nicomachean Ethics* and applied to the organization
of the state in the *Politics*. It argues against the view that for Aristotle
distributive justice is only a means to promoting the common good
and against the view of Martha Nussbaum that Aristotle understands
the common good in a special way that leads to egalitarian conclusions.]

MCREYNOLDS, Phillip, "Nussbaum's Capabilities Approach: A
Pragmatist Critique," *Journal of Speculative Philosophy*. 2002;
16(2): 142-150.

[The essay briefly outlines Martha Nussbaum's capabilities approach
as articulated in *Women and Human Development*. It notes similarities between Nussbaum's list of basic capabilities and John Dewey's
approach to ethics. Both approaches view as distinctively human our
sociality and intelligence. However, although the capabilities
approach makes progress in attempting to consider women's actual
situations in formulating an account of what it means to be completely human, her approach overlooks the ways in which the concept
of "the human" has been deployed against oppressed peoples. The
essay argues that this problem can be mitigated by focusing upon
ethics as inquiry.]

MERCHANT, Carolyn, *The Death of Nature* (San Francisco: Harper &
Row, 1980).

[The Scientific Revolution of the Renaissance involved a mechanis-
tic view of nature which exploited women and nature. The feminine
aspect of humanity and the universe has thereby been "killed," hence
the title of the book. After examining modern science and its mascu-

line world-view, the author offers alternatives for rediscovering traditional values, which will help restore the balance between the masculine and feminine that has been missing since the time of Leibniz and Newton.]

MOODY-ADAMS, Michele M., "The Virtues of Nussbaum's Essentialism," *Metaphilosophy*. October 1998; 29(4): 263-272.

[This paper shows that Nussbaum's Aristotelian essentialism effectively combines resources for constructive social criticism (even in "traditional" societies) with concern for the concrete particulars of realized ways of life. Many critics of Nussbaum's views have failed to appreciate its many virtues in this regard. Yet Nussbaum's confidence in the broad possibilities of internal social criticism demands a better account of the moral openness of human cultures than anything Nussbaum has herself provided. Even Nussbaum's reading of Aristotle—as well as the ethical antirelativism on which it depends—demands a richer account than Nussbaum has so far offered of the essential openness of human world interpretations.]

MULGAN, Richard, "Was Aristotle an 'Aristotelian Social Democrat'?," *Ethics: An International Journal of Social, Political, and Legal Philosophy*. October, 2000; 111(1): 79-101.

[There are reasons for questioning whether Aristotle laid the basis for social democracy and the redistributive state. He excludes manual workers from participation in the good life even though they have the natural potential for the life of virtue. His support for equality in distribution does not extend to equalizing unequal opportunities. Though free choice is an essential component of virtue, Aristotle does not support a liberal pluralist state.]

NUSSBAUM, Martha, "Aristotle, Feminism, and Needs for Functioning" in *Feminist Interpretations of Aristotle*, Cynthia A. Freeland, ed. (University Park: Pennsylvania University Press, 1998).

NUSSBAUM, Martha, "Aristotle, Politics, and Human Capabilities: A Response to Antony, Arneson, Charlesworth, and Mulgan," *Ethics: An International Journal of Social, Political, and Legal Philosophy*. October 2000; 111(1): 102-140.

NUSSBAUM, Martha, "Capabilities and Human Rights" in *Global Justice and Transnational Politics*, Pablo De Greiff, ed.. (Cambridge MA: MIT Press, 2002; 117-149).

NUSSBAUM, Martha, "Conversing with the Tradition: John Rawls and the History of Ethics," *Ethics: An International Journal of Social, Political, and Legal Philosophy*. January 1999; 109(2): 424-430.

NUSSBAUM, Martha, "Equity and Mercy," *Philosophy and Public Affairs*. Spring 1993; 22(2): 83-125.

NUSSBAUM, Martha, "Feminism and Internationalism," *Metaphilosophy*. January 1996; 27 91-2): 202-208.

NUSSBAUM, Martha, "The Future of Liberal Feminism," *Proceedings and Addresses of the American Philosophical Association*. November 2000; 74(2): 47-79.

NUSSBAUM, Martha, "Human Functioning and Social Justice: In Defense of Aristotelian Essentialism," *Political Theory: An International Journal of Political Philosophy*. May 1992; 20(2): 202-246.

NUSSBAUM, Martha, "Lesbian and Gay Rights: Pro" in *The Liberation Debate: Rights at Issue*, Michael Leahy, ed. (New York: Routledge, 1996).

NUSSBAUM, Martha, "Morality and Moral Perception" in *Constructions of Practical Reason: Interviews on Moral and*

Political Philosophy, Herlinde Pauer-Studer, ed. (Stanford: Stanford University Press, 2003; 113-127).

NUSSBAUM, Martha, "Political Animals: Luck, Love, and Dignity," *Metaphilosophy*. October 1998; 29(4): 273-287.
[Card argues well that our vulnerability to luck is intertwined in the very conditions of moral agency. We can see the merit of her approach even more clearly by turning to some difficulties the Stoics have in preserving dignity while removing vulnerability. Richardson is correct to suggest that love itself can animate concern for all humanity; I also agree with him that institutions must play a major role in any solution to problems of inequality between nations. Although the "capabilities approach" offers an attractive account of one part of the goal of just political institutions, combining, as Moody-Adams suggests, respect for difference with a commitment to universal norms. I now believe that the capabilities account should be combined with a form of Rawlsian political liberalism that protects spaces within which citizens may pursue the good as they understand it.]

NUSSBAUM, Martha, "Public Philosophy and International Feminism" in *What is Philosophy?*, C. P. Ragland, ed. (New Haven: Yale University Press, 2001; 121-152).

NUSSBAUM, Martha, "Rawls and Feminism" in *The Cambridge Companion to Rawls*, Samuel Freeman, ed. (Cambridge: Cambridge University Press, 2003; 488-520).

NUSSBAUM, Martha, *Sex and Social Justice* (New York: Oxford University Press, 1999).

NUSSBAUM, Martha, "Symposium on Amartya Sen's Philosophy: 5 Adaptive Preferences and Women's Option," *Economics and Philosophy*. April 2001; 17(1): 67-88.

NUSSBAUM, Martha, "Women and Cultural Universals" in *Pluralism: The Philosophy and Politics of Diversity*, Maria Baghramiau, ed. (New York: Routledge, 2000).

NUSSBAUM, Martha, *Women and Human Development: The Capabilities Approach* (Cambridge: Cambridge University Press, 2000).

NUSSBAUM, Martha, and SEN, Amartya, eds., *The Quality of Life* (New York: Oxford University Press, 1993).

[Contributors to this volume include G. A Cohen, Amartya Sen, Christine Korsgaard, Dan W. Brock, James Griffin, Hilary Putnam, Lorenz Kruger, Michael Walzer, Ruth Anna Putnam, Thomas Scanlon, Sissela Bok, Charles Taylor, Martha Nussbaum, Susan Hurley, Julia Annas, Margarita Valdes, Onora O'Neill, John E. Roemer, Paul Seabright, M. S. Van Praag, Siddiq Osmani, Derek Parfit, and Christopher Bliss.]

PIERCE, Christine, "AIDS and Bowers versus Hardwick," *Journal of Social Philosophy*. Winter 1989; 20(3): 21-32.

PIERCE, Christine, "Gay Marriage," *Journal of Social Philosophy*. Fall 1995; 26(2): 5-16.

PIERCE, Christine, *Immovable Laws, Irresistible Rights: Natural Law, Moral Rights, and Feminist Ethics* (Lawrence: University Press of Kansas, 2000).

PHILLIPS, Anne, "Feminism and Liberalism Revisited: Has Martha Nussbaum Got It Right?," *Constellations: An International Journal of Critical and Democratic Theory*. June 2001; 8(2): 249-266.

QIZILBASH, Mozaffar, "Well-Being and Despair: Dante's Ugolino," *Utilitas: A Journal of Utilitarian Studies*. July 1997; 9(2): 227-240.

[This paper considers three sorts of accounts of the quality of life. These are (1) capability views, due to Amartya Sen and Martha Nussbaum, (2) desire accounts, and (3) the prudential value list theory of James Griffin. Each approach is evaluated in the context of a tale of cannibalism and moral decay: the story of Count Ugolino in Dante's *The Divine Comedy*. It is argued that the example causes difficulties for Sen's version of the capability approach, as well as for desire accounts. Nussbaum's version of the capability approach deals with the example better than Sen's. However, it fails adequately to accommodate pluralism. I suggest that James Griffin's account of well-being deals well with this example and accommodates pluralism. I suggest that, of the views considered, Griffin's is the best account of the quality of life.]

RICHARDSON, Henry S., "Nussbaum: Love and Respect," *Metaphilosophy*. October 1998; 29(4): 254-262.

[This article details how Martha Nussbaum has heightened the potential tension between love and respect, flagged by Kant, by strengthening what each requires. She elaborates the particularism and disruptiveness of love while insisting on a cosmopolitanism of respect. The article suggests that dealing with this tension will require developing a more detailed theory of institutional justice, one that can extend to the international arena.]

RUHL, Lealle, "Natural governance and the governance of nature: The hazards of natural law feminism," *Feminist Review*. Autumn 2000; 66: 4-24.

RUSSELL, J. S., "Okin's Rawlsian Feminism? Justice in the Family and Another Liberalism," *Social Theory and Practice: An International and Interdisciplinary Journal and Social Philosophy*. Fall 1995; 21(3): 397-426.

[This paper rejects Susan Moller Okin's attempts to enlist a Rawlsian theory of justice to challenge the gender-structured character of modern societies. It argues that the methodology of the original position prevents this, mainly because of its emphasis on protecting pluralism and liberty, but also because of Okin's own arguments regarding the limitations of the original position. The paper concludes that Okin's feminism fits more readily within a neo-Aristotelian framework of the sort that has recently been defended by Martha Nussbaum and others. A precursor to Okin's and Nussbaum's feminism is noted in the feminism of the liberal Aristotelian philosopher, L. T. Hobhouse.]

STRAUS, Nina Pelikan, "Rethinking Feminist Humanism," *Philosophy and Literature*. October 1990; 284-303.

TRAINA, Cristina L. H., "Baird Callicott's Ethical Vision: Response to Baird Callicott," *American Journal of Theology and Philosophy*. January 1997; 18(1): 81-87.

[Baird Callicott's proposal for a global ethic resonates with important elements of Roman Catholic moral theology: for example, a willingness to connect fact and value in universal norms, and a concern for the interdependent common good. Environmental ethics that follow his model must also avoid the historic natural law pitfalls of making universal claims prematurely, excluding minority viewpoint, and eclipsing the rights of individuals or marginal groups. Yet, lacking a detailed vision of environmental flourishing, Callicott's ethic may also lack the power for prophecy and therefore, for generating convincing common standards. Theologians must address this problem as well.]

TRAINA, Cristina L. H., *Feminist Ethics and Natural Law: The End of the Anathemas* (Washington, D. C.: Georgetown University Press, 1999).

[After carefully scrutinizing Aquinas's moral theology and analyzing trends in both contemporary feminist ethics and twentieth-century Roman Catholic moral theology, Traina shows that a truly Thomistic natural law ethic provides a much-needed holistic foundation for contemporary feminist ethics. She proposes an innovative union of two supposedly antagonistic schools of thought, a new feminist natural law that would yield more comprehensive moral analysis than either existing tradition alone.]

TRAINA, Cristina L. H., "Passionate Mothering: Toward an Ethic of Appropriate Mother-Child Intimacy" in *The Annual of the Society of Christian Ethics 1998: Volume 18*, John Kelsay, ed. (Chicago: DePaul University, 1998).

[Women's informal accounts of their experience, news reports, and psychological and endocrinological studies concur that maternal-infant relations are inevitably erotic, if not explicitly sexually charged. In a culture that both affirms pursuit of "natural" pleasure and condemns overt eroticism in any relationship between unequals, maternal erotic experience is problematic. This essay gathers insights from the literatures of psychoanalysis, naturalism, maternal practice, and victim advocacy, as well as the Christian theological ethics of Lisa Sowle Cahill, Christine E. Gudorf, and Bonnie J. Miller-McLemore to construct a tentative descriptive and prescriptive account of maternal eroticism.]

TUANA, Nancy, "Aristotle and the Politics of Reproduction" in *Engendering Origins*, Bat-Ami Bar On, ed. (Albany: SUNY Press, 1994).

[I argue that Aristotle's theories of generation illustrate the depiction of difference in terms of "lack" common to the Western metaphysical tradition. I contend that Aristotle's characterization of woman as a deviation from the "true form" of humanity was an unsupported axiom and the culmination of a gradual process of degradation of the female generative powers in ancient and classical Greece.]

TUANA, Nancy, *The Less Noble Sex: Scientific, Religious, and Philosophical Conceptions of Woman's Nature* (Bloomington: Indiana University Press, 1993).

[Ranging over literature from philosophy, cosmology, theology, and science, *The Less Noble Sex* examines theories of woman's nature to illustrate the way scientific literature, from Classical times through the late nineteenth century, has been influenced by, and has in turn influenced, religious and philosophical tenets. The analysis provides a framework for understanding the persistence of the Western view of woman as inferior. Equally important, scientific, philosophical, and religious reasoning on this topic is juxtaposed to illustrate how disciplines affect and reinforce one another. Tuana documents that science has been "gendered", that is, that sexist biases have permeated the structure of science.]

TUANA, Nancy, "The Weaker Seed: The Sexist Bias of Reproductive Theory," *Hypatia: A Journal of Feminist Philosophy*. Spring 1988; 3: 35-59.

[The history of reproductive theories from Aristotle to the preformationists provides an excellent illustration of the ways in which the gender/science system informs the process of scientific investigation. In this essay I examine the effects of the bias of woman's inferiority upon theories of human reproduction. I argue that the adherence to a belief in the inferiority of the female creative principle biased scientific perception of the nature of woman's role in human generation.]

TUANA, Nancy, *Woman and the History of Philosophy* (St. Paul: Paragon House, 1992).

TUMULTY, Peter, "Aristotle, Feminism, and Natural Law Theory," *New Scholasticism*. Autumn 1981; 55: 450-464.

[Notoriously, Aristotle maintained the inferiority of women, and is also often cited as one of the sources for natural law theory. The paper argues that his pattern of moral reasoning which requires logically an appeal to the characteristics of women is exactly right, and that that same conception of moral reasoning requires affirming the equality of women given today's knowledge. In contrast, alternative moral theories must base their arguments for the equality of women on grounds other than the intrinsic characteristics of men and women.]

WARREN, Karen J., ed., *Ecological Feminist Philosophies* (Bloomington: Indiana University Press, 1996).

[This volume includes contributions by Stephanie Lahar, Karen Warren, Chris Cuomo, Deane Curtin, Roger King, Deborah Slicer, Robert Sessions, Val Plumwood, Victoria Davion, Patricia Jagentowicz Mills, Patrick Murphy, and Jim Cheney.]

FEATURE

AUSTIN'S COMPLEMENTARY JURISPRUDENCE*
Avner Levin

INTRODUCTION

Ever since H. L. A. Hart rejected what has been called the "sanction theory of law" in favor of his concept of law as a union of primary and secondary rules it has been largely thought that John Austin's jurisprudence can no longer offer an insightful answer to the question of law's nature. Hart uncovered the deficiencies of the "sanction theory" as a complete jurisprudence, and showed that to think that all that there is to law is sanctions, commands, sovereign and subjects, is simplistic at best. The model of the "sanction theory" "failed to do justice to the complexity of the facts," as Hart put it, and was therefore an inadequate theory of law.[1] Yet Austin himself stated that:

> It has often been affirmed that "right is might," or that "might is right." But this paradoxical proposition (a great favourite with shallow scoffers and buffoons) is either a flat truism affectedly and darkly expressed, or is thoroughly false and absurd.[2]

Are the "sanction theory of law" and Austin's jurisprudence one and the same? I will argue in this article, as indeed Hart acknowledged, that they are not.[3] To distinguish between them I will call the version of legal positivism that Hart criticized Austinism.[4] It is an extreme form of legal positivism, no doubt, but it is also not Austin's theory of law. That it is not

---

* I would like to thank David Dyzenhaus, Leslie Green, Alan Brudner and Timothy Endicott for their comments on earlier versions of this article.

[1] H. L. A. Hart, *The Concept of Law* (P. Bullock and J. Raz Eds., 2nd ed. With postscript, Oxford: Clarendon Press, 1994), 91.

[2] John Austin, *Lectures on Jurisprudence* (5th ed. rev. London: John Murray, 1885), 284.

[3] For more on the idea that Hart does "injustice" to Austin see Robert Moles, *Definition and Rule in Legal Theory* (Oxford: Blackwell, 1987).

[4] See William Morison, *John Austin* (Stanford: Stanford University Press, 1982), 148-177, on the popularity of what I call Austinism, and its deviations for Austin's actual views.

Austin's theory of law is demonstrated not only by the substantive positions it holds, but also by its methodological approach to the law, inasmuch as this methodological approach can be ascertained from Hart's criticism.

In order to substantiate my claim I will briefly review Austinism's familiar substantive features and methodology as discussed and criticized by Hart. I will show how Austinism's substantive positions are, as Hart claimed, Austin's positions taken to the extreme, and how they do not accurately represent Austin's theory of law. I will then argue that this conclusion is strengthened by the realization that Austin's methodology is not the extreme positivist approach of Austinism. Not only is Austin's theory of law distinct from Austinism but it offers an answer, or at least indicates the building blocks from which an answer may be constructed to contemporary debates within jurisprudence as to the manner in which legal theory is conducted. The debate today is, of course, described in terms that were not used by Austin at the time, and some of Austin's terminology has been neglected over the years as well. I shall attempt to describe Austin's position by using contemporary terms as accurately as possible, while keeping in mind that phrases such as the "external point of view," "internal aspect," and various classifications of legal theories were introduced by Hart as he was criticizing Austinism, and by later philosophers of law.

Hart characterized his approach to legal theory as "general and descriptive,"[5] and it has been an approach rejected, at least in its descriptive aspirations, by other philosophers of law such as Dworkin, Finnis and Raz.[6] Austin, I will argue, offered an approach to legal theory and a form of jurisprudence that can best be understood as a complementary theory of law, a theory of law that coherently incorporates within it elements from what would today be called the stated approaches of Hart on

[5] Hart, *The Concept of Law*, 239-240.

[6] See most recently Ronald Dworkin, *Hart's Posthumous Reply* (1994), 2 and Joseph Raz, "Two Views on the Nature of the Theory of Law: A Partial Comparison" 4 *Legal Theory* 249 (1998), 273 (footnote 38 to text).

the one hand, and Dworkin, Finnis and Raz on the other, to produce a complete and sophisticated jurisprudence.

AUSTINISM

Austinism's substantive positions and methodology were outlined by Hart in his critique of the sanction theory of law. The three main substantive features of Austinism are first, that all laws are general commands; second, that these commands emanate from a constant and supreme sovereign; and third, that members of society are in habitual obedience to the sovereign.[7] The main methodological feature of Austinism is that it is conducted from a perspective external to law, so that it does not account for the manner in which law figures in the lives of members of society who accept it as their standard of behavior.[8] Austinism is therefore a positivist theory of law, in more senses than one. It is a positivist theory of law in its substantive positions by awarding the status of law only to those dictates that emanate from a specific social source—the sovereign. The identification and verification of law begin and end with Austinism's sovereign so that what the law is is in no way influenced by what the law should be. At the same time the status of law is also conveyed by the substantive requirement for habitual obedience, so that the sovereign's law must rest on a basis of effective legal practice. The prominence of habitual obedience as a necessary requirement for law to fulfill indicates that Austinism is also a positivist theory of law in its methodology. By constructing itself on an external observation of legal reality Austinism attempts to proceed along the lines of scientific inquiry, limiting itself to empirical and objective legal data (to the extent that these terms are meaningful in nonscientific legal context) and hoping to distill from them illuminating features of law. While this methodology allows Austinism to construct what it considers are the essential and distinctive features of law on the empirical and objective basis of legal practice, it also runs the risk of over-simplifying the law, reducing it to a few essential elements that would form a skeletal model, rather than a theory

---

7 Hart, *The Concept of Law*, 16-25. Strictly speaking, the third can be deduced from the first two, yet it allowed Hart to distinguish his approach from Austinism methodologically as well.

8 Ibid., 90.

of law. In such a manner commands are often misunderstood as threats, the notion of the sovereign is reduced to that of a dictator, and habitual obedience turns into fear of sanctions. Hence, as Hart acknowledged, the somewhat inaccurate result is the sanction theory of law that he set out to criticize:

> ... we shall state and criticize a position which is, in substance, the same as Austin's doctrine but probably diverges from it at certain points if we have not hesitated where Austin's meaning is doubtful or where his views seem inconsistent to ignore this and to state a clear and consistent position. [9]

Hart's criticism of Austinism is as well known as are the simple tenets of Austinism above. First, some laws are not, and cannot be characterized as, commands. Some laws, for instance, confer powers on officials or individuals.[10] Second, the notion of a continuously supreme sovereign does not exist. In modern societies the sovereign is neither continuous nor supreme but is rather subject to the rule of law as well.[11]

Third, habitual obedience fails to capture the perspective of those members of society that accept the law as their standard of behavior. Their perspective is one internal to the law, and Austinism's external analysis of law cannot successfully incorporate it.[12] In all these Hart did not take issue with Austinism's substantive positions, although their end result is a shift from Austinism's substantive idea of law as the vessel of political hierarchy to Hart's idea of law as a hierarchy of rules. In his criticism, however, Hart simply adopted Austinism's methodology to the extent that he evaluated Austinism according to the accuracy with which it described the features of law, and then set out to show how Austinism's substantive positions did not fit the very objective and empirical obser-

[9] Ibid., 18.
[10] Ibid., 28.
[11] Ibid., 70.
[12] Ibid., 40.

vations about the law they were meant to rely on.[13] Hart was able to conclude in such a manner that:

> ... at various crucial points, the simple model of law as the sovereign's coercive orders failed to reproduce some of the salient features of a legal system. To demonstrate this we did not find it necessary to invoke (as earlier critics have done) international law or primitive law which some may regard as disputable or borderline examples of law; instead we pointed to certain familiar features of municipal law in a modern state, and showed that these were either distorted or altogether unrepresented in this over-simple theory.[14]

Hart's argument, in a sense, was that he simply carried out Austinism's descriptive mission better, and that unlike Austinism he was able to correctly identify those features of law that explain and illuminate it, and that are, (a point equally as important) backed up by the reality of contemporary legal systems as well. So Hart did not argue so much with Austinism's methodology as he did with the manner in which it was carried out. It was appropriate, according to Hart, to attempt to understand how law functions in society on the basis of general descriptions. It was wrong, however, to conduct these observations from a vantage point so external to law it could not hope to capture those features of law that were crucial to understanding the manner in which law functions in society:

> It is sometimes urged that by recasting the law in a form of a direction to apply sanctions, an advance in clarity is made, since this form makes plain all that the "bad man" wants to know about the law. This may be true but it seems an inadequate defence...Why should not be law equally if not more concerned with the 'puzzled man' or 'ignorant man' who is willing to do what is required...? Or with the 'man who wishes to arrange his affairs'...? It is of course very important, if we

13 Whether these descriptive aspirations remained at the basis of Hart's methodology in his construction of his own theory of law is arguable. I tend to think that they did, and so apparently did Hart, at least judging by his comments both in his preface and in his postscript to *The Concept of Law*, but they can certainly be understood differently. See for example Stephen Perry, "Hart's Methodological Positivism," 4 *Legal Theory* 427 (1998), as well as the first chapter of John Finnis, *Natural Law and Natural Rights* (Oxford: Clarendon Press, 1980.)

14 Ibid., 79.

> are to understand the law, to see how the courts administer it
> when they come to apply its sanctions. But this should not lead
> us to think that all there is to understand is what happens in
> courts.[15]

A legal theorist, according to Hart, could therefore gather his general and descriptive observations of law from two points of view. The legal theorist interested in understanding the role law plays for all members of society:

> ...may, without accepting the rules himself, assert that the
> group accepts the rules, and thus from outside refer to the way
> in which *they* are concerned with them from the internal point
> of view.[16]

A legal theorist who accepts Austinism's methodology, however, is an observer who is:

> ... content merely to record the regularities of observable
> behavior in which conformity with the rules partly consists,
> and those further regularities, in the form of the hostile reac-
> tion, reproofs, or punishments with which deviations from the
> rules are met.[17]

And so Austinism's methodology limits it to reproducing the manner in which:

> ...the rules function in the lives of certain members of the
> group, namely those who reject its rules and are only con-
> cerned with them when and because they judge that unpleasant
> consequences are likely to follow violation... What the exter-
> nal point of view, which limits itself to the observable regular-
> ities of behavior, cannot reproduce is the way in which the
> rules function as rules in the lives of those who normally are
> the majority of society. These are the officials, lawyers, or pri-
> vate persons who use them...as guides to the conduct of social
> life...[18]

[15] Ibid., 40.
[16] Ibid., 89 (emphasis in original.)
[17] Ibid., 89.
[18] Ibid., 90.

Austinism is therefore a positivist theory of law both methodologically and substantively. Substantively, it argues that law cannot be determined by morality since it identifies as law only those dictates of the sovereign that society habitually obeys. Law's source is social, not moral. This position is known today as the Sources Thesis and stands at the basis of Raz's theory of positivism,[19] (although Raz's social sources are different from Austinism's sovereign). Methodologically, it argues that the explanation of law must rest on general and descriptive observations of law, conducted by an observer not necessarily subject to the law. Austinism precludes therefore, by means of its method, any meaningful explanation of the manner in which law is normative for members of society. And Austinism's substantive positions are the direct outcome of its methodology. It reduces, by means of its methodology, law's complex role in society to a simple model of coercive order backed by threats, since all its methodology allows for is the external explanation of patterns of behavior. The rival explanation of law as it applies to those accepting it as standards of behavior is ignored. In doing so, contended Hart, it relinquishes the role of legal theory:

> One of the difficulties facing any legal theory anxious to do justice to the *complexity of the facts* is to remember the presence of both these points of view and not to define one of them out of existence. Perhaps all our criticisms of the predictive theory of obligation may best be summarized as the accusation that this is what it does to the internal aspect of obligatory rules.[20]

For Hart, therefore, Austinism's biggest failure was not in its strict adherence to the separation of law and morals, but in its methodological failure to remain faithful to that other tenet of positivism, to provide a theory of law as it is, rather than as it should be. Austinism failed to provide a theory of law along Hart's general, and more importantly, descriptive goals. A more accurate description of law was provided, according to Hart, by the concept of law as a union of primary and secondary rules

[19] The Sources Thesis argues that all law is based on social sources. See most recently Joseph Raz, *Ethics in the Public Domain* (Oxford: Clarendon Press, 1994), 194-195.

[20] Hart, *The Concept of Law*, 91 (emphasis added).

resting on their acceptance as standards of conduct by at least the officials of society. Yet I will argue that Austin, as opposed to that rudimentary model of law that Hart criticized and which I have called Austinism, was very much aware of the complex role law had to play within society. In the following section I will argue that Austin attempted to formulate a jurisprudence that went beyond "hard" or "exclusive" positivism, as Austinism's positions are now called, to explore and provide an account of law's normative basis.

AUSTIN

Austinism was characterized by Hart as a doctrine having little interest in whatever moral basis law might have, indeed in whatever social basis law might have other than the brute force of coercion. Austin was convinced, however, that a theory of law is the result of an inquiry into law, morality, and the relationship between them, and constructed his jurisprudence accordingly.[21] In discussing Austin's substantive positions and his methodology I will therefore endeavor to show not only that they exceed the limitations of Austinism, but that they reflect Austin's general conviction about jurisprudence. That is not to say that Austinism cannot be deduced from Austin's jurisprudence. But it is, I will argue, a very limited deduction, and one that does not follow in the direction Austin had intended for legal theory.

Austin constructed the relationship between law and morality according to his general definition of law:

> A law...may be said to be a rule laid down for the guidance of
> an intelligent being by an intelligent being having power over
> him.[22]

Unlike Austinism's understanding of laws, Austin acknowledges that laws in general are meant to guide behavior, although they do represent a relationship of power as well. But this definition is not limited to laws based in social sources. It rather serves to distinguish between the various normative systems with which Austin was familiar. There was of course

[21] Austin, *Lectures on Jurisprudence*, 16.
[22] Ibid., 86.

law that was set forth by God to humans, which Austin called Divine Law.[23] Then there was law that was set forth by people in power to other people, whom they controlled. This law was called by Austin "positive law."[24] These two examples, according to Austin, were the only instances that fully followed his definition. There were, however, other cases of "law." Following the above definition, these cases were again divisible. First, there was the case where the so-called rule was laid down by people who were actually not in power, and second, there was the case where the so-called rule was not required to be backed by power at all, but by some other force, such as convention, habit, or public opinion. These two cases were labeled by Austin jointly as "positive morality." "Positive" signifies that these decrees were not God's and "morality" signifies that these decrees were not proper rules.[25]

Although law and morality play equal parts in the working of society (in a manner Austin had yet to specify) it was clear that they were not conceptually similar. "Positive morality" was distinct from "positive law," although there was a great deal of confusion, widespread belief, or "improper usage" to suggest otherwise. "Positive morality" was a term defined almost exclusively negatively, i.e., not law and not God-given. Note that Austin did not employ the notion of "critical morality," since for him the notion of evaluative criteria, developed by humans, and by which human laws and human actions are measured, was incomprehensible. There was only one such standard, and it was law of God:

> For the name *morality* (or *morals*) when standing unqualified or alone, denotes indifferently either the following objects: namely, positive morality *as it is*, or without regards its merits; and positive morality as *it would be*, if it conformed to the law of God, and were, therefore, deserving of *approbation*.[26]

There are therefore three terms which relate to each other: positive law, positive morality, and Divine Law, where the first two constantly aspire to the third, and there is no fourth term, such as "critical morality" by

[23] Ibid., 86.

[24] Ibid., 86.

[25] Ibid., 87.

[26] Ibid., 87-88 (emphasis in original).

which they could be measured. Divine Law played for Austin the role which critical morality today plays for some legal theorists in the debate between positivism and anti-positivism. The relationship between these three terms holds the key to the understanding of Austin's jurisprudence in a context wider than Austinism.

It turns out, for instance, that Austinism's notion of laws as commands was put forward in more detail by Austin. True, in the context of positive law as defined above Austin stated that "Every *law* or *rule* is a *command*."[27] The notion of "command" incorporated within it the relationship of power previously mentioned in the definition of laws in general:

> A command…is a signification of desire…distinguished from other significations of desire by this peculiarity: that the party to whom it is directed is liable to evil from the other, in case he comply not with the desire.[28]

Yet although commands are regularly backed by power Austin did not think that sufficient to turn them into rules of law. Of equal importance was the requirement that rules apply to behavior over time, that rules guide behavior and form patterns of habitual behavior. A command addressing a specific and particular situation could not be considered, therefore, a rule:

> Again, suppose the sovereign to issue an order, enforced by penalties, for a general mourning, on occasion of a public calamity. Now, though it is addressed to the community at large, the order is scarcely a rule, in the usual acceptation of the term.[29]

The act of parliament designating Remembrance Day, on the other hand, was a rule, since the action it called for was repetitive. The regularity of behavior manifesting itself in rules which are followed was paramount, echoing the linguistic connection between the meaning of a rule as a standard of conduct to be followed, and a pattern of regular conduct which can be objectively assessed, as in the case of determining the rules of

[27] Ibid., 88.

[28] Ibid., 89.

[29] Ibid., 95.

physics. Moreover, Austin believed that patterns of regular behavior in nature were termed "rules" precisely because it was incomprehensible to the human mind that any form of regular behavior may occur without the force of an originating (Divine, in nature's case) command.[30]

Not only did Austin consider the habitual aspect of rules more important to their determination in such cases than their portrayal of political power, he was willing to acknowledge, within the domain of positive law, that some laws are not necessarily backed by political power at all. These exceptions to Austin's definition included three main categories. First, there were "declaratory statutes," these being acts of parliament, which were not commands but explanations of previous commands.[31] Second, there were "permissions," acts of parliament that repealed previous acts, or negated previously imposed duties. These, of course, could not be defined as commands as well.[32] Third, there were "imperfect laws," not in any moral sense, but in the sense that they lacked an element of the definition of law proposed by Austin. Most commonly these rules lacked the element of sanction, and therefore were commands that were not backed adequately by power, and hence could not be labeled as commands at all.[33]

Other potential exceptions were not really exceptions to the description of rules as commands as far as Austin was concerned, and he set out to show why. Acts that created or affirmed rights were not an exception but commands because they simultaneously imposed obligations on others to respect these rights.[34] Custom, or customary law, could also be defined as a command of the sovereign, not by way of its origin, which was truly in the general observation of it by subjects, but by way of its enforcement, when it was adopted by a judge, who was ultimately a representative of the sovereign, a vessel of the sovereign's power. The fact that the sovereign was always able to reverse a judicial endorsement of custom as law, indicates that the sovereign's tacit acceptance of such

[30] Ibid., 207.
[31] Ibid., 98.
[32] Ibid., 99.
[33] Ibid., 100.
[34] Ibid., 100.

decisions amounted to backing them by power as the sovereign's own commands.[35]

So it becomes increasingly difficult to equate Austin with Austinism. While one can understand how Austinism might include the above "pseudo-exceptions" within its definition of law, there is no readily available reason to incorporate within Austinism those exceptions that Austin viewed as genuine. Some believe that the only reason Austin dealt with these exceptions to begin with is the fact that they were treated as law by Bentham, whom Austin did not wish to contradict.[36] While there may be some truth to such an observation Austin's treatment seems also to indicate that his approach to legal theory was not Austinism's approach. Certainly, from the pragmatic aspect of conducting legal science Austin believed that:

> ... the space occupied in the science by these improper laws is comparatively narrow and insignificant. Accordingly, ... I shall limit the term law to laws which are imperative, unless I extend it expressly to laws which are not.[37]

This is one part of an explanation which indicates that, although Austin wished to arrive at generalized conclusions about the law, he did not perceive his understanding of law as the construction of a model of law, and he certainly did not intend to construct the simplistic model of Austinism at the expense of a more comprehensive description of law. On the contrary, it seems that Austin was unable to deny those acts that were, in actual practice, referred to as "laws" by a vast majority of practitioners, a status as actual "laws."

The social fact established by such practice was too strong for Austin to ignore, since he set forth with the task of classifying and understanding the data available to him in society and its habits. Austin's approach and methodology are revealed in this instance, when, after noting that "declaratory statutes" are actually forms of interpretation, Austin goes on to say:

[35] Ibid., 102.

[36] Morison, *John Austin*, 65-66.

[37] Austin, *Lectures on Jurisprudence*, 103 (emphasis in original).

> But, this notwithstanding, they are frequently styled laws; ...
> They must, therefore, be noted as forming an exception to the
> proposition 'that laws are a species of commands. [38]

There is no theoretical justification in this passage to include such statutes as "rules," merely Austin's descriptive methodology at work. It is only the evidence that "declaratory statues" are recognized as rules in practice, which promotes them to the status of an exception.

Merely on the basis of the above analysis of Austin's notion of rules I can tentatively conclude that Austin's jurisprudence cannot be equated with Austinism. Austin's treatment of exceptions to his definition of rules as rules nonetheless, based on a widespread social practice to this effect, breaks with the principle of Austinism as explained by Hart. Significantly, it indicates that Austin's approach to legal theory recognized the "complexity of the facts" of legal reality, as Hart put it, and that Austin was attempting to accommodate legal reality within his theoretical framework, rather than pigeonhole it into a "simplistic model" of law. Austin's notion of sovereignty, which I shall now discuss, serves to strengthen this tentative conclusion.

The supreme and continuous sovereign is law's social and singular source according to Austinism. Superiority was a requisite for Austin's definition of laws in general, and hence for his definition of positive laws as commands as well.[39] Yet once again, as it was with the portrayal of positive laws as commands, superiority was not the begin-all and end-all of Austin's notion of sovereignty. The distinction between an orderly society and one controlled by arbitrary force focused, once again, on the importance of social practice and habit (but not exclusively on observable patterns of behavior, as I shall discuss below). A sovereign was in existence in society according to Austin only once society had recognized the sovereign's superiority by establishing a pattern of habitual obedience to the sovereign's dictates.[40] The essence of superiority was to be found not in political might, but in society's practical recognition of the sovereign

[38] Ibid., 98.
[39] Ibid., 96.
[40] Ibid., 220.

as such. The sovereign itself could be a person or a determinate group of people, not habitually obeying anyone else of course.[41]

The notion of habitual obedience, in the context of serving as a requisite for the sovereign's social existence, has to be explored in greater detail. So long as obedience was manifested in observable patterns of behavior Austin was content, for instance with only a majority of society habitually obeying the sovereign, and did not require, as one might deduce from Austinism, that all members of society obey the sovereign continuously.[42] In the conditions of sovereignty Austin allowed therefore for the possibility that a dictator would be a sovereign according to his theory of law, but did not equate sovereignty with dictatorship. Indeed, Austin went through a variety of regimes, ranging from "monarchies" to "democracies" and discussed how they conform to his understanding of sovereignty.[43] Lest this be insufficient, Austin proceeded with an examination of the different branches of government within these regimes, again pointing out how different mechanisms of power delegation were compatible with his notion of sovereignty.[44] Austin therefore concluded:

> If a *determinate* human superior, *not* in a habit of obedience to a like superior, receive habitual obedience from the *bulk* of a given society, that determinate superior is sovereign in that

[41] Ibid., 220. The group had to be defined since that was the way Austin distinguished between the sources of positive morality and the sources of positive law:

> For example, A law set or imposed by the *general* opinion of barristers condemns the sordid practice of hugging or kissing attorneys. And as those whose opinion or sentiment sets the so called law are an indeterminate part of the determinate body of barristers, they form a body uncertain and incapable of corporate conduct. But in case a number or portion of that uncertain body assembled and passed a resolution to check the practice of hugging, that number or portion of that uncertain body would be, by the very act, a certain body or aggregate. It would for a determinate body consisting of the determinate individuals who assembled and passed the resolution. A law imposed by general opinion may be the cause of a law in the proper acceptation of the term. (Ibid., 189-190)

[42] There were many political possibilities here, which Austin discussed at great length. Ibid., 222-234.

[43] Ibid., 239.

[44] Ibid., 243.

society, and the society (including the superior) is a society
political and independent. To that determinate superior, the
other members of society are *subject*.[45]

Yet if the basis of sovereignty is habitual obedience it is only reasonable
to assume that habitual obedience limits sovereignty's supremacy in some
way once habitual obedience is understood as a notion comprised of more
than observable patterns of behavior. Austin declared that "Supreme
power limited by positive law, is a flat contradiction in terms."[46] But
although Austinism ends there, the key to understanding Austin's
jurisprudence is that such a statement is just its starting point. There are
restraints, Austin acknowledged, which exist upon sovereigns (here too is
Austin's descriptive methodology at work). Those restraints that prevent
sovereigns from abusing their position emanate from the domain of positive morality, which although not positive law, is nevertheless a powerful force in an orderly society.[47] Indeed, this is another example of
Austin's conviction that the two are connected:

> Positive law (or *jus*), positive morality (or *mos*), together with
> the principles which form the texts of both, are the inseparably
> connected parts of a vast organic whole.[48]

Austin's conclusion that the sovereign is constrained not by law but
by morality, and at the same time that such a constraint is no weaker for
its origins, is significant. Those holding on to Austinism could view it as
another step Austin was forced to take down a path he did not wish to
complete, the recognition of the important role positive morality (and its
normative basis) has to play in supposedly legal matters. On the other
hand, the issue of sovereignty allows us to realize that for Austin, to
determine the province of jurisprudence was not to imply (as Austinism
might) that everything that lay outside the borders of jurisprudence was
unimportant. For Austin, determining the province of jurisprudence
allowed a clear, true and objective perspective on the ways in which soci-

45 Ibid., 221 (emphasis in original). I should note that Austin went on to discuss and
justify the use of these terms, despite their inherent vagueness. Ibid., 227-230.

46 Ibid., 263. Needless to say, those members of a sovereign body are of course bound
by the law as individuals. Ibid., 272.

47 Ibid., 264.

48 Ibid., 16.

ety functions. Once one realized where, according to Austin, the true boundaries of law lay one could realize the important role morality has within society, and how law and morality are equal components in the functioning of an "orderly society."[49] And the broader conclusion that can be drawn with respect to Austin's philosophy is that Austin did not view the description of positive law as paramount, with an inquiry into its non-social sources, to the extent that these existed at all within his jurisprudence playing second fiddle, at best. Rather, Austin attempted to balance both approaches within his theory of law and his understanding of how law operates in society. It is this overall balanced approach that led Austin to the realization that supreme power can be limited, although not by positive law but by positive morality (with its origins, as I shall discuss, in Divine Law), and it is here where the normative basis of the notion of habitual obedience must be explored. In order to do so I must first discuss how Austin perceived the relationship between positive morality and Divine Law.

Austin believed that Divine Law as such was unobtainable directly by humans, yet all sought to understand it as fully as possible.[50] Such understanding could be obtained in two ways, neither of which was fully accepted by Austin. One was the theory of utility, or utilitarianism, serving, in lieu of absolute knowledge, as "the index to His will."[51] The reasoning behind the theory of utility is as follows: Although one does not know the content of Divine Law fully, one does know that God is good and therefore that God wants all to be happy. All rules that increase common happiness are then closer to Divine Law than rules that diminish common happiness. As a result, all should make it their principle (the principle of utility) to always follow and enact rules that promote happiness, rather than rules that do not:

> Inasmuch as the goodness of God is boundless and impartial,
> he designs the greatest happiness of all his sentient creatures:
> he wills that the aggregate of their enjoyments shall find no
> nearer limit than that which is inevitably set to it by their finite
> and imperfect nature. From the probable effects of our actions

[49] That this conclusion has to be drawn at all attests to the degree of success that the identification of Austinism with Austin has had. It is, in effect, Moles' thesis.

[50] Austin, *Lectures on Jurisprudence*, 123.

[51] Ibid., 140.

> on the greatest happiness of all, or from the tendencies of
> human actions to increase or diminish that aggregate, we may
> infer the laws which he has given, but has not expressed or
> revealed.[52]

An emphasis should be placed on the utility of rules, as establishing patterns of behavior, rather than on one-time actions, when assessing the change to general happiness. As an example, Austin argued that any single theft may increase happiness, but thefts in general diminish it, and so should be prohibited.[53] Only when one observes the effects of a single action recurring again and again is one able to make a true judgement of its utility. Rules are also important since they enable one to avoid potentially complex calculations of happiness and misery before every action one takes. If a rule exists governing an action one is contemplating, one should determine whether the rule, rather than the course of action as such, promotes happiness. That is an easier task for one to fulfill. Moreover, one can safely assume that such deliberations have already taken place with respect to many of the rules that govern life. Hence, one can follow rules in life and safely assume that one is increasing happiness just by abiding with the law, avoiding calculations and deliberations at the same time.[54] As an "index to His will" however, the principle of utility is imperfect. Since the only way of learning about Divine Law is based on observations of actual human conduct, and since the principle of utility is also based on human conduct, one has in it, at best, an approximation to an approximation.[55] Although the effects of such imperfections can be mitigated, for example by increasing awareness among members of society to the ideas of morality and the principle of utility, they cannot be nullified.[56] Another way must be found in order to determine Divine Law as it truly is. This attempt is based on the notion of a "moral sense" or "moral instinct," a human faculty that guides one, as a compass, to the knowledge of the law of God. This human faculty is based neither on education and moral awareness nor on the principle of utility. It is an instinct,

[52] Ibid., 106.
[53] Ibid., 107.
[54] Ibid., 114.
[55] Ibid., 141.
[56] Ibid., 141.

a sense, i.e., an immediate response to any moral question that faces one without pause for deliberation or thought. Austin's example is to suppose a person was brought up in isolation and without education, only to be set loose upon the world. This person might encounter people with food, and kill them for it. Then, other people would attack this person for the same food, and she would kill them to protect her life. Austin postulated that this person would feel remorse at the first murder, but not at the second, and the difference in feelings can only be attributed to her moral instinct, since from a standpoint of utility they are the same, and since she was brought up without any knowledge of right and wrong.[57] Since there is no logical explanation for this difference one is forced to account for it by ways of assuming a moral sense, or a moral instinct:

> Certain inscrutable sentiments of approbation or disapprobation accompany our conceptions of certain human actions. They are not begotten by reflection upon the tendencies of the actions which excite them, nor are they instilled into our minds by our intercourse with our fellow-men. They are simple elements of our nature. They are ultimate facts. They are not the effects of causes, or are not the consequents of antecedents, which are open to human observation.[58]

If indeed such an instinct exists, then by virtue of being an instinct, a basic, natural, perhaps biological trait that one possesses, a moral instinct or moral sense must, like other senses one enjoys, be both instantaneous, and common.[59] In exactly the same manner that sights or sounds cast their impressions upon the senses so must it be with moral situations. Moral opinions must therefore form immediately, and moreover, in the same manner that a noise is heard by all, or an odor detected by all, so must a moral situation be comprehended by all. Having stated these two consequences, Austin recognized that they may not exist, at least not without some modifications. First, Austin noted that many moral decisions are not made instantaneously, but on the contrary, only after much deliberation and hesitation.[60] Moreover, even if everyone were to decide on all moral

---

[57] Ibid., 146-148.
[58] Ibid., 149.
[59] Ibid., 150.
[60] Ibid., 151.

problems without hesitation, such social conduct would not be proof, in itself, that a moral instinct exists, since it could be, for example, the result of excellent moral education.[61] Second, it was clear to Austin that members of society do not react all in the same way to moral situations, and that the proper response to certain situations has not only been in disagreement, but the subject of much moral debate:

> The respective moral sentiments of different ages and nations and of different men in the same age and nation, have differed to infinity. This proposition is so notoriously true, and to every instructed mind the facts upon which it rests are so familiar, that I should hardly treat my readers with due respect if I attempted to establish it by proof.[62]

The two conclusions, which are drawn from the assumption of the existence of a moral instinct, raise doubts whether such an instinct exists in the first place, and at most allow it to exist only in limited fashion. On the other hand, Austin turned to the study of moral sense because his examination of utilitarianism proved the principle of utility problematic as well. Austin was now moved to offer a synthesis of these two competing theories, one that he hoped would salvage the best in both, and discard their respective problems. Austin labeled this synthesis the Intermediate, or Compounded Hypothesis:

> According to an intermediate hypothesis, compounded of the hypothesis of utility and the hypothesis of a moral sense, the moral sense is our index to *some* of His tacit commands, but the principle of general utility is our index to *others*.[63]

Austin proposed that although the notion of a moral instinct was proven to be wrong when society in its entirety was discussed, or the entire civilized world, it had some truth to it when the moral responses of a limited body of persons, similar to each other in education, values, or social stature were examined. A moral sense, therefore, serves in those matters that pertain to one's "class," or to a "class" closely similar, with which

61 Ibid., 151.

62 Ibid., 152.

63 Ibid., 153 (emphasis in original).

one shares much of one's background and beliefs.[64] In those matters one is able to decide quickly and without hesitation. One possesses common ground and common moral values with other members of one's "class" that allows moral judgement to be almost instinctive. Not all moral matters pertain to one's "class," however, and some questions one has to decide upon involve members of other societies, or people with a background vastly different. In such instances one's moral sense will point in one way, while the moral sense of others will inevitably point in a different direction. These are the cases where all should rely on the principle of utility, which incorporates a method of analysis comprehensible to all. The principle of utility serves, therefore, where a common background, with the people whose actions one is assessing, is lacking. These may be foreigners, for example, or historical figures, or members of a different social level, and so on.[65]

The Compounded Hypothesis accounts in such a manner for my strong moral feelings toward certain actions in certain circumstances, as well as the possibility that others will have equally strong, but different attitudes, at the same time. Multicultural issues are good examples for the ways in which the Compounded Hypothesis works (even though on many occasions these issues are referred to a court of law). For instance, should members of particular faiths, such as Jews or Sikhs, be allowed to wear their religious headdresses when joining an organization such as the army or the police, which mandates a headdress of its own? In such an example one "class" or community, perhaps even the majority of society, may employ its moral sense to find that such religious deviations should not be allowed. On the other hand, the religious minorities have an equally strong moral sense that they should be allowed to retain their headdresses. Moral instinct fails members of society in this matter, so according to the Compounded Hypothesis they are to turn to the principle of utility, and attempt to determine which rule would bring to society greater happiness, maintaining the rule that only police hats are allowed, or opting for a different rule, which would allow for many different religious headdresses. The Compounded Hypothesis serves therefore as the link

[64] Ibid., 153.
[65] Ibid., 153.

between positive morality and Divine Law.[66] Since Austin's notion of sovereignty was based upon a social practice of habitual obedience, and constrained by positive morality, the inescapable conclusion is that habitual obedience is based on, or limited in some way by, Divine Law, through the mechanism of the Compounded Hypothesis. Here indeed is what Austin had to say on the workings of an ideal society:

> Supposing that a given society were adequately instructed or enlightened, the habitual obedience to its government which was rendered by the bulk of the community, would exclusively arise from reasons bottomed in the principle of utility.[67]

In an enlightened society one finds therefore, almost "out of the blue" to those holding on to Austinism, a relationship between the foundations of a legal system and morality, offered by none other than Austin himself. In an enlightened society, members of society obey the law because they morally approve of it. Law is the means by which the principle of utility is followed, since the principle of utility is at the basis of every enlightened society:

> The proper purpose or end of a sovereign political government, or the purpose or end for which it ought to exist, is the greatest possible advancement of human happiness...[68]

Here, therefore, is a characterization of law that can hardly be thought to comply with Austinism's dictates, although it certainly, as I have labored to show, follows Austin's chain of reasoning: Most, but not all, laws are commands, the commands of a sovereign. However, the sovereign rules supreme because members of society have a habit of obeying the sovereign. And furthermore, members of society develop a habit of obedience not because the sovereign's commands are backed by sanctions but because considerations of utility instruct them to do so. To summarize

[66] Austin contended as well that the Compounded Hypothesis accounted for the existence of two separate bodies of law, natural law, which originated in the moral sense, and positive law, which arose out of utilitarian calculations. Accepting solely the principle of utility, or solely the idea of a moral sense, would fail to account for why both these bodies of law existed. Ibid., 154-155.

[67] Ibid., 293.

[68] Ibid., 290.

this chain of reasoning, in an enlightened society members of society obey the law because they are morally obligated to do so.[69] According to Austin, a law must enjoy social consensus ("habitual obedience" by the "bulk of society") in order for it to be properly called law, and such widespread consensus can only be based on an attitude towards the law by those subject to it that takes law's moral basis into account, and not for example, on some threats made by a lone gunman or a group of thugs.

What of actual societies, which are, one is to assume, not so enlightened? Can one infer from the chain of reasoning in the case of an enlightened society to regular societies? Austin thought some qualifications had to be made:

> Since every actual society is inadequately instructed or enlightened, the habitual obedience to its government which is rendered by the bulk of the community is partly the consequence of custom...or...partly the consequence of prejudices...[70]

Here are two important qualifications. In an ordinary society, habitual obedience is based in a number of sources, not only in the principle of utility. The first example noted by Austin is custom. Some members of society simply follow the law because they have already developed a habit, or have inherited a habit, to do so.[71] For members of an ordinary society custom bears independent weight as a reason for acting in a certain way, simply because it has been so well established over a lengthy period of time, and they do not pause to scrutinize its origins. Second, people follow the law because of their "prejudices," a term that meant for Austin reasons that could not be traced back to considerations of utility.[72] As examples of such considerations, Austin gave the love of the monarchy, or the love of the ideal of democracy. In other words, some people may follow the law because the sovereign is democratic, and they

[69] Strictly speaking considerations of utility created a moral obligation only in certain situations. In other situations moral obligations were created by one's "moral instinct." Ibid., 153.

[70] Ibid., 294.

[71] The argument basing habitual obedience on custom, or simply put, on habits formed at an earlier point in time, is a circular argument, for one is looking for a reason why such a habit would have formed in the first place.

[72] Austin, *Lectures on Jurisprudence*, 294.

approve of democracy, or because the sovereign is from the House of Windsor whom they adore, without taking any other considerations into account.

Nevertheless, both reasons of custom and "prejudice" could be linked through the Compounded Hypothesis outlined above, if not to the principle of utility then to the idea of "moral sense" and through it to the normative basis of Divine Law. And these qualifications allowed Austin to proceed with his argument. Even in an ordinary society, the principle of utility still has a role to play:

> But though that habitual obedience is partly the consequence of custom, or though that habitual obedience is partly the consequence of prejudices, it partly arises from a reason bottomed in the principle of utility. It partly arises, from a perception by the generality or bulk of the community, of the expediency of political goverment.[73]

In an ordinary society members do not go about reflecting on the principle of utility, but rather they follow the law because it is what they have been taught by their elders, or because they prefer order to chaos for their personal reasons, or they have other reasons for doing so altogether, such as the love of their queen. Whatever these may be, Austin did not think that the notion of obedience is fully accounted for by the "extremely external" observation that members of society follow the law because of its power to inflict harm upon them. Moreover, the habit of obedience seems inseparably connected to a moral attitude, minimally stated as the preference of government to anarchy, which is "a reason bottomed in the principle of utility."[74] It is this connection, rather than some other descriptive element of the law, which is common to all systems of law:

> The habitual obedience to the government which is rendered by the bulk of the community, partly arises,...in almost every society, from...a perception...of the utility of political government...And this is the only cause of the habitual obedience...which is common to all societies, or nearly all societies.[75]

[73] Ibid., 294.

[74] Ibid., 294.

[75] Ibid., 295.

Indeed, in a footnote Austin stated:

> It is possible to conceive a society in which legal sanctions
> would lie dormant or in which quasi government would mere-
> ly recommend, or utter laws...[76]

Of course, if a society already approves of its sovereign there is moral
approval above and beyond the simple dislike of anarchy, and consequently, little need for sanctions.[77] If, however, society disapproves of its
sovereign, there are two possibilities. First, that one is dealing with an
enlightened society, in which case the dissatisfaction is based upon considerations of utility, implying that the sovereign has no moral basis.[78]
The second possibility is that one is dealing with an ordinary society, in
which case no conclusion can readily be drawn from the fact that society
is unhappy with its sovereign to the sovereign's moral standing.[79] In the
case of an ordinary society such unhappiness is based in many different,
even contradictory sources (such as custom or prejudices) so that members of society are led to the conclusion that the continuing reign of the
present sovereign is preferable to an uncertain political situation in the
sovereign's absence (i.e., anarchy). This utility-based decision is
strengthened by fear of the sanctions imposed by the sovereign. In other
words, in such a situation, society fears not only the results of a change
in sovereignty, but the sanctions it will have to endure through a period
of disobedience as well. Fear of sanctions is incorporated in such a manner into more general considerations of utility, but overall, the complexity of carrying out the Compounded Hypothesis in the moral evaluation of
the sovereign of an actual society leaves the extent to which sovereignty
is based, ultimately, upon Divine Law, unclear. What is clear is that for
Austin, as opposed to Austinism, sovereignty, law's social source, is
based upon positive morality and through it at least partially upon morality. Far from being a "sanction theory of law" Austin's jurisprudence has
proven more faithful in its substantive positions to Hart's methodological

[76] Ibid., 294 (footnote 29 to text).

[77] Ibid., 297. Unfortunately, and perhaps realistically, Austin thought of this possibility as highly unlikely, or "ridiculously false."

[78] Ibid., 297. Again, enlightened societies are scarce.

[76] Ibid., 297.

aspirations than could have been expected from it on the basis of Hart's criticism of Austinism. In the concluding section I will discuss the methodology that enabled Austin to do so, a far cry from Hart's characterization of Austinism's "extremely-external" observational point on law.

CONCLUSION—AUSTIN'S METHODOLOGY

Contemporary discussion of jurisprudential methodology roughly divides it into two approaches.[80] There is an approach to jurisprudence that has been labeled pragmatic or descriptive, and there is an approach to jurisprudence that has been labeled normative, constructive or prescriptive.[81] These approaches do not necessarily correlate with the various substantive positions grouped under the banners of positivism on the one hand, and natural law or anti-positivism on the other. Unless they are crude attempts it is usually the case that theories are comprised of elements of both approaches, and efforts made at understanding theories such as Hart, Finnis, Dworkin, or Raz's within the confines of one methodological approach usually end up as an exercise in pigeonholing. Nevertheless, it could be said that descriptive jurisprudence attempts to understand law without reference to the values of other normative systems, whereas prescriptive jurisprudence contends that understanding law is meaningful only once its normative basis is understood as well. Accordingly, Dworkin and Finnis hold a more prescriptive approach to jurisprudence, while Hart laid claims to the descriptive approach.[82] I have

[80] See Jules Coleman, *The Practice of Principle* (Oxford: Oxford University Press, 2001) as well as *The Oxford Handbook of Jurisprudence and Philosophy of Law* (forthcoming), 237-315; David Dyzenhaus, "Positivism's Stagnant Research Programme," 20 *Oxford Journal of Legal Studies* 703 (2000); Stephen Perry, "The Varieties of Legal Positivism," 9 *Canadian Journal of Law and Jurisprudence* 361 (1996) and more recently "Hart's Methodological Positivism," 4 *Legal Theory* 427 (1998); Gerald Postema, "Jurisprudence as Practical Philosophy," 4 *Legal Theory* 329 (1998) as well as "The normativity of Law," Ruth Gavison (ed.), *Issues in Contemporary Legal Philosophy* (Oxford: Clarendon Press, 1987); Joseph Raz, "Two Views on the Nature of the Theory of Law: A Partial Comparison" 4 *Legal Theory* 249 (1998); Wilfred Waluchow, *Inclusive Legal Positivism* (Oxford: Clarendon Press, 1994), 30, 165 and more recently "In Pursuit of Pragmatic Legal Theory" 15 *Canadian Journal of Law and Jurisprudence* 125 (2002).

[81] For the latest mapping of the debate see Waluchow, "In Pursuit of Pragmatic Legal Theory" 127-137.

[82] But on the success of his claims see Perry, "Hart's Methodological Positivism," 467.

no room to argue for it here, but Raz, although undoubtedly descriptive in his methodological aspirations, can be thought of as a prescriptive theorist with his construction of law on the basis of authority.[83] Hart has argued that his approach is general as well as descriptive, yet it seems a theory need not be descriptive in Hart's sense in order to provide a general explanation of law. Both Dworkin and Raz, for instance, understand their work as an attempt to create a general jurisprudence, yet not necessarily a descriptive one (in Hart's sense of the notion). Dworkin is unapologetic about his views that law should be understood through its purpose, while Raz differentiates between his task of identifying the essential features of law and Hart's task of describing the general features of law.[84] Within this debate Austin's theory has long been thought to be the paradigmatic example of descriptive jurisprudence.[85] That is a widespread, and I hope I have already begun to indicate, incorrect assumption that emphasizes Austin's descriptive methodology at the expense of both his general aspirations and his interest in understanding law's normative basis.

It is true that Austinism, constructed from its "extremely-external" observational point is an exercise in descriptive jurisprudence that shows no interest in understanding law's normative basis. But, as I have made clear above, Austin's substantive theoretical positions about law are not only not the principles of Austinism, but are positions impossible to reach from a point of view so external to law and so indifferent to its normative basis. However, before attempting to understand Austin's methodology in terms of the contemporary discussion it is important to understand that Austin was primarily driven by the methodological concerns of his period. Those concerns were of course different from the methodological interests of today. Austin perceived the field of legal studies at his time as confused and disorganized. This was a field where according to Austin concepts such as laws or rules had no well-defined meaning and were

[83] Law's claim of authority is its "essential" feature according to Raz. See Raz, *Ethics in the Public Domain*, 221.

[84] See for example Dworkin, *Law's Empire* (Cambridge: Belknap Press, 1986), 98 or Ronald Dworkin "Reply" in Marshall Cohen (ed.), *Ronald Dworkin and Contemporary Jurisprudence* (Totowa: Rowman and Allanheld, 1983), 258; Raz, "Two Views on the Nature of the Theory of Law," 267-268.

[85] Perry, "Hart's Methodological Positivism," 467.

subject to broad and careless interpretations, where no common ground existed between scholars which could promote the understanding of law's social role. Austin saw his work, therefore, as first and foremost an establishment of such a common ground, as building a structure of legal terminology which could be agreed upon, and subsequently arriving at an objective (in this context taken to mean a generally agreed upon) understanding of positive law and positive morality. This work, according to Austin, was two-staged. First, one had to determine what the playing field was, so to speak. Second, one had to spell out once the borders of the field were well defined what the rules of the game were. The borders of positive law and positive morality had to be traced before the various legal terms could be analyzed and comprehended in their social and moral context, and before the relationship between positive law and positive morality, and through it morality, could be understood:

> ...positive law (or law, simply and strictly so called) is often confounded with objects to which it is related by *resemblance*, and with objects to which it is related in the way of analogy: with objects that are also signified, *properly* and *improperly*, by the large and vague expression law. To obviate the difficulties springing from that confusion I begin...with determining the province of jurisprudence, or from distinguishing the matter of jurisprudence from those various related objects: trying to define the subject of which I intend to treat, before I endeavour to analyse its numerous and complicated parts.[86]

In other words, Austin first took it upon himself to describe law, and only then to provide an understanding of law based on this description.

Much of the confusion from which legal theory suffered according to Austin could be traced back to a methodological failure to separate the description of law from the understanding of its social purposes on the one hand, and its normative basis on the other. And much of the confusion from which the reading of Austin as Austinism suffers could be traced back to the misconception that Austin's jurisprudence is only about determining the boundaries of positive law. Indeed, in the part of his lectures where he attempted to determine those boundaries Austin sought to describe what law is and not prescribe what it should be:

---

[86] Austin, *Lectures on Jurisprudence*, 86 (emphasis in original).

> ...the science of legislation (or of positive law as it ought to
> be) is not the science of jurisprudence (or of positive law as it
> is)...[87]

In determining the boundaries of positive law Austin perceived his project as one of practical research rather than as one of normative evaluative considerations. He set out to offer an orderly framework for the mul-
titude of laws, rules and other "legal facts" that already existed within the
legal system, keeping in mind, however, that such a framework would
necessarily fail unless all, or nearly all, of these components of the legal
system were accounted for. It was clear to Austin that such a framework
had to be sufficiently rich to serve as the basis for a theory of law that
understood law in normative terms.

It is because of this desire to construct a rich framework of legal concepts that perhaps the most immediate observation that can be made about
Austin's methodology is of Austin's use of conceptual analysis. Austin
generally proceeded about it in a meticulous fashion. Every concept he
employed was first defined by simpler concepts, until concepts that
appeared, at least to Austin, to have a common, non-contested meaning,
were employed.[88] These concepts were then used for two purposes: first,
to aid in the definition of more complicated concepts, and second, to
assist in the construction of a theory of law.[89] Although there is much that
can be said (and indeed, has already been said) against the method of conceptual analysis in general, it is important to understand that despite the
criticism that can be leveled against this aspect of Austin's methodology,
it is part and parcel of his overall two-staged methodological attempt.

In contemporary terms Austin's methodology, while based in the concerns and techniques of his time, can be viewed therefore as a combination of both descriptive and prescriptive jurisprudence. His attempt to
firmly define the domains of positive law and positive morality, and only
then to engage in the construction of their relationship, can be viewed not

[87] Ibid., 83 (emphasis in original).

[88] Of course, as I have noted above Austin was aware of the inherent vagueness that at
least some concepts suffer from.

[89] It is almost as if Austin attempted single-handedly to establish a body of what
Dworkin calls preinterpretive law, upon which he would later construct his particular conception of law. See Ronald Dworkin, *Law's Empire*, 65-66.

only as a product of the disorderly field of legal theory he perceived but also as a product of Austin's unique and complementary methodological approach. Since Austin has been equated so often with Austinism, I have stressed his inquiry into the normative basis of law at the expense of his more familiar (and as I have argued, wrongly understood) positions on positive law. I should now caution against the opposite reading of Austin. Austin's methodology does not consist solely of the evaluation of law in light of its social and moral purposes (a method to which Dworkin's jurisprudence applies) and of the explanation of law through its normative basis. My argument is that Austin's methodology is a complementary combination of both and that Austin attempted (and of course his degree of success is debatable), in the methodological goals he set out for himself, to equally pursue both descriptive and prescriptive methodologies in order to produce a general theory of law.

There can be a conflict, of course, between a theory's aims and methods. Sometimes a theory aiming to be general must sacrifice descriptive details, and sometimes a theory's understanding of law's normative basis runs the risk of losing its general appeal. Austin attempted to achieve a balance between these competing meta-theoretical concerns within his jurisprudence as well, as is reflected in his understanding of positive law being comprised of a general definition and valid exceptions, discussed above. Austin's desire to provide a general account of positive law resulted in his observation that all laws are habitually obeyed commands. It is this method that leads to Austinism, to the theory of law as enforced by coercion, and to the strict separation of law and morals implied by an understanding of law as coercive orders backed by threats. Austin's desire to provide a descriptive account of positive law is the outcome of his understanding of positive law as distinct from Divine Law in the sense that it must reflect and be based upon sensory data. This method forced Austin to consider all those exceptions "out there" in contradiction to his general account of positive law as relevant and pertinent, since they had the force of simply existing. Any theorist who holds that fitting theory to practice is important would face the same dilemma, of attempting to account for myriad facts on the one hand, and presenting a general theory of the way law functions, on the other. Furthermore, Austin's desire to provide an account of the normative basis of positive law culminated in

his analysis of the normative foundations of the social practice of habitual obedience.

So Austin's jurisprudence attempted to complement general, descriptive and prescriptive methods. As a perhaps more successful example of
how these methodological approaches work in tandem within Austin's
jurisprudence, consider indeed Austin's notion of habitual obedience and
compare it on the one hand with Hart's competing notion of acceptance,
that was motivated by Hart's descriptive methodology and disinterest in
law's normative basis, and on the other hand with Dworkin's notion of
integrity, motivated by Dworkin's method of constructive interpretation.[90] Hart's notion of acceptance was the outcome of his methodological approach, aimed at providing a description of law from an external
point of view and wishing to remain silent on law's normative basis, yet
nonetheless wishing to take into account law's normative functions as
well (the only function Hart would contemplate was the guidance of
behavior). The inevitable tension this approach created within Hart's theory of law has of course been discussed at great length and it has been
also pointed out that Hart's notion of acceptance is ill suited for accounting for law's normative basis.[91] It remains an open question whether Hart
intended his theory of law to account for law's normative basis or not,
although it seems based on Hart's statements that he did not.[92] While the
normative acceptance of law (i.e., its acceptance as a standard of conduct)
by members of society at large is possible within Hart's theory it is by no
means necessary. A legal system is efficacious, according to Hart, even if
only its officials accept the law in such a sense, while the rest of society
continues to habitually obey the law.[93] Yet this is, of course, habitual obedience according to Austinism, i.e. the mere observance of regular patterns of behavior that conform to the law's dictates. It is not based in any
normative evaluation of the law, indeed it is meant to be understood as
carrying less normative meaning than the notion of acceptance, in itself
invested with already little normative significance.

While Hart was content (perhaps) methodologically with jurisprudence merely providing an account of law's necessary efficacy condi-

[90] A comparison could be made to Raz's notion of authority as well.

[91] Postema, "The Normativity of Law," 95.

[92] Hart, *The Concepts of Law*, 257.

[93] Ibid., 114-116.

tions, opponents of Hart's methodological approach, such as Dworkin, claim that it is only through their methodology that an inquiry into the normative basis of law is facilitated. Dworkin's method of constructive interpretation, with its emphasis on law's normative basis at the expense of its efficacy conditions, leads to Dworkin's notion of integrity.[94] Law should provide the justification of coercion according to Dworkin, and only a legal system with integrity achieves this paramount purpose of law.[95] For Dworkin every coercive system is necessarily based on some moral values, and the degree by which obedience is morally approved reflects society's endorsement of the coercive order in force.[96] Law enjoys the greatest integrity when based upon morality and different systems enjoy different degrees of integrity, based upon their moral evaluation. However, the moral evaluation of law is of course independent of the manner in which members of society perceive law. It is conducted according to the principles of morality as Dworkin understands them.[97] Furthermore, Dworkin's evaluation is limited to the adjudicative branch, and is the result of his more general moral and political theory, so that the value of integrity towards which legal systems should strive, and that some legal systems enjoy in varying degrees, is determined largely by the actions and values held by law's officials. Indeed, Raz has gone so far as to criticize Dworkin for providing a theory of adjudication, rather than a theory of law.[98] Since Dworkin's methodology dictates his theory of law as a product of his more general political and moral theories it is of no surprise that the actual normative attitude displayed by members of various societies towards their law does not really influence his understanding of law.[99]

[94] On the value of integrity in adjudication see Dworkin, *Law's Empire*, 96.

[95] Dworkin, *Law's Empire*, 188.

[96] Dworkin, "Reply", 258.

[97] Dworkin believes of course in the demonstrability of moral values. See Ronald Dworkin, "Objectivity and Truth: You'd Better Believe It" 25 *Philosophy and Public Affairs* 87 (1996).

[98] Raz, "Two Views on the Nature of the Theory of Law," 282.

[99] For instance, even if all the members of an evil society morally approve of their law Dworkin would still not be moved to the conclusion that theirs is truly a legal system, as opposed to a coercive one. Dworkin, "Reply," 260.

Only a complementary methodology is able to successfully incorporate within one theory of law an inquiry into both its conditions of efficacy and its normative basis. It leads to a realization that a theory of law is
needed which will explain the attitude most members of society appear to
have towards the law in any given society. How is it, for instance, that
Western legal systems typically enjoy the endorsement of most of their
members and do not rely merely on their officials' acceptance?[100] A theory of law equally interested in describing law and understanding law's
normative basis should explain, across a spectrum of legal systems, the
notions of the law according to members of society, and the law for members of society, drift apart. At one end of the spectrum, presumably in
Western democracies, there is no difference between the law according to
members of society and the law for members of society. At the other end
of the spectrum, in the "wicked" systems, the law according to members
of society is not the law for members of society.[101] Austin's jurisprudence
achieved this purpose through the notion of habitual obedience.

Austin's determination of the normative basis of law (the principle of
utility) led him to an inquiry into the sources of habitual obedience to the
law. Compared with Hart's notion of acceptance Austin was the one who
sought within his jurisprudence to understand law as based on society's
perception of the good inherent to government. It was Austin who did not
shy away from positioning these public perceptions squarely in the
domain of morality, and not in the realm of normative acceptance. Austin,
not Hart, complemented his descriptive discussion of law with an inquiry
into law's normative basis. As a general basis for a theory of law habitual obedience seems superior to both Hart and Dworkin's emphasis of the
role of officials, since it is an attitude which is exhibited by all members
of society (in varying degrees). It is not conceptually limited, like the idea
of acceptance or integrity, to one part of society. It therefore provides a
better description of the state of affairs in many legal systems than the one
provided by Hart's notion of acceptance or Dworkin's notion of integrity

[100] This is an empirical claim not everyone agrees with. See Leslie Green, "Who
Believes in Political Obligation" in John Sanders and Jan Narveson (eds.), *For and
Against the State* (Lanham: Rowman and Littlefield, 1996), 1.

[101] For a discussion of "wicked" legal systems see David Dyzenhaus, *Hard Cases in
Wicked Legal Systems* (Oxford: Clearendon Press, 1991).

that are both, in their minimal requisites, limited to a group of officials within society. Compared with Dworkin's notion of integrity, in every society according to Austin a necessary component of the basis of habitual obedience was a normative one, the principle of utility. It may be that not every legal system promoted happiness as it should, yet every legal system was necessarily based on principles of morality (considerations of utility) however minimal they may have been.[102] The degree by which obedience was morally approved reflected society's endorsement of the coercive order in force, and according to Austin, obedience that was based solely upon considerations of utility reflected a society that was enlightened, although actual societies varied in the degree by which obedience was based upon utility. Yet Austin's habitual obedience was not integrity by another name. Questions of interpretation, of the preferred conception of law that would enhance law's integrity, were not questions that Austin perceived as open to the discussion and resolution of the adjudicative branch. Judges were merely that, a subordinate branch of the sovereign government,[103] and their individually independent motives were of little consequence for a theory that attempted to explain how the law is identified, applied and followed in general. Habitual obedience reflected the normative basis of law in society at large, while Dworkin's evaluation is limited to the adjudicative branch, and is the result of his more general moral and political theory. Austin's habitual obedience was partially based as well on positive morality in actual societies, acknowledging in such a manner as legitimate systems that were perhaps not adequately based on principles of morality.

A case in point is the example of "wicked" systems. Dworkin rejects such systems as legal (except in a very limited preinterpretive sense), while for Hart questions of their legitimacy as opposed to their existence were distinct.[104] Austin, through the notion of habitual obedience, was able to account for such a system as legal by means of his simple yet powerful descriptive analysis of coercive systems, and allow for the possibility of varying degrees of moral legitimacy in different legal systems.

[102] Austin thought that legal systems could promote more happiness through codification. Austin, *Lectures on Jurisprudence*, 653.

[103] Ibid., 531.

[104] See Dworkin, *Law's Empire*, 102-104, *Hart's Posthumous Reply*, 26-27 and generally Dworkin, "Reply"; Hart, *The Concept of Law*, 270.

Austin was therefore not led, on the one hand, to discount certain coercive systems as non-legal as does Dworkin. But he was also not led, on the other hand, to conclude that the legitimacy of coercive systems is a matter not suitable for legal theory, as did Hart. Austin's theory allowed him to engage in a moral evaluation of its descriptive elements, without discounting them as 'mistakes' that had to be explained away. Similarly, Austin was not forced by his discussion of law's normative basis to deny the descriptive basis of his theory. Austin's methodology complemented inquiries into law's normative basis with inquiries into law's mechanism.

My discussion of Austin's methodology as it is revealed through his substantive positions on law, morality and habitual obedience does not intend to argue that Austin's jurisprudence is more complete or extensive than the philosophies of law that I have compared it to. What I hope this discussion achieves is the realization that Austin's jurisprudence is more sophisticated and subtle than the Austinism it has long been taken to be. Furthermore, Austin's complementary methodology significantly adds to the contemporary discussion of the goals and methods of legal theory. Let there be no mistake, a complementary theory of law is more than a suggestion that one should accommodate Hart, Finnis, Dworkin or Raz's positions in every jurisprudential debate. It is a jurisprudential effort in its own right, a theory of law attempting to understand law both through an institutional approach and an internal approach, from both a descriptive and a normative perspective, in a coherent manner. Austin certainly did not set out to write a complementary theory of law. The very notion and debates it is meant to address, of course, had not yet been developed in his time. I hope to have successfully argued, however, that Austin can be understood as providing at the very least a rudimentary notion of a complementary theory of law in his approach to the law. Austin's theory of law carried to its extreme, Austinism, is a model of law rather than a theory of law. It sacrifices the nuances of description and prescription in favor of generalizations that are not entirely accurate. A complementary theory of law would be able to account for the details of description and prescription in a way that a model of law cannot.

It is in this manner that Austin's jurisprudence can be understood as a complementary theory of law. For Austin was unique in his ability to combine strong, descriptive methodology on the one hand (which led to Austinism), with its goal of an explanation of the way law functions in society, through legal systems which are structured in specific ways, together with an approach which focused on explaining the law through its normative basis and social and moral purposes, an inquiry into the purposes some of his descriptive observations serve, on the other. Austin's jurisprudence was the location where these approaches were able to coexist not as rival theories, not as projects with different agendas, but as one project which was able to account for, and allocate correctly, questions of description and normative questions to the respective areas of jurisprudence to which they were most appropriate. Austin's theory of law was committed neither to providing an exhaustive description of law nor to a program that takes the risk of pronouncing much of legal practice, and many systems considered by their participants to be legitimate, a normative "mistake" in light of the purposes or essential features of law it identifies.

Moreover, Austin's jurisprudence did not undermine its descriptive observations as a result of its inquiry into law's normative basis, and at the same time it did not abandon its inquiry into the normative basis of law in favor of a singular descriptive approach. It was a project which was interested in the description of law, in the determination of the province of positive law, yet a project which was also interested in how the law conforms to our notion of good, in how the law serves as a justification for action, a project which was interested in the rationale for boundaries it determined to exist between law and morality,[105] and which found that rationale in the particular purpose of the advancement of happiness. That particular foundation (which was strongly based in Austin's descriptive observations) enabled Austin to refrain from the disqualification of descriptive elements on the one hand, yet enabled a moral evaluation inseparable from a theory of law on the other. That particular basis constituted Austin's theory as a rudimentary form of a complementary theory of law, and traced the course that a contemporary complementary theory of law must follow.

Consider the contemporary discussion within positivism over the incorporation of morality as a possible source of law in line with Hart's notion of a rule of recognition. Raz's understanding of law through its

---

[105] Austin, *Lectures on Jurisprudence*, 82.

claim to authority leads him to reject morality as a source of law and per-
mits him to understand it, at best, as offering guidelines for judicial dis-
cretion.[106] Methodologically, Raz argues for a description of law based on
law's essential features as Raz understands them, not as participants in the
legal system understand them (although Raz claims that his understanding of law conforms to the common understanding of the law, he does not
think that it is necessarily dependent on the common understanding of
law). Countering this methodology is inclusive positivism with its pragmatic tendencies.[107] Translated into a desire to theoretically accept and
account for features that members of society perceive as legal and legitimate, inclusive positivism argues that morality is a possible source of
law.[108] And while positivism has been taking Hart's rule of recognition as
a granted feature of contemporary legal systems, anti-positivism has been
contesting this very assumption, and countering it with an alternative
description of law.[109] So the debate has been an interesting one, both
methodologically and substantively. It is of course mere speculation and
an extrapolation of Austin's jurisprudence to attempt to discern Austin's
possible position within this debate, yet it is an exercise that shows the
continuing importance of a complementary methodological framework.
Austin clearly distinguished between morality (Divine Law) and positive
law as two separate "'provinces." Yet this strongly motivated descriptive
distinction was but a necessary step in Austin's methodology towards the
formulation of the relationship between positive law and positive morality based on the principles by which Divine Law was to be ascertained,
the normative basis upon which the "vast, organic whole" of law was
founded. It seems to me, therefore, that Austin suggested another way in
which morality can serve as a source of positive law, perhaps not exactly
in line with contemporary versions of inclusive positivism. Rather than
begin with an already contested descriptive framework (the idea that

---

[106] Raz, *Ethics in the Public Domain*, 213.

[107] As summarized by Waluchow, "In Pursuit of Pragmatic Legal Theory" 129-134.

[108] Despite their distinctions, Waluchow's "inclusive positivism" and Coleman's
"incorporationism" are versions of positivism that permit a system's rule of recognition
to refer to moral criteria. Hart labeled these versions "soft" positivism. See most recently
Hart, *The Concept of Law*, 250; Waluchow, *Inclusive Legal Positivism*; Coleman, *The
Practice of Principle*.

[109] Dworkin, *Hart's Posthumous Reply*, 20.

there is broad social convention that identifies and determines law, i.e., a rule of recognition) and attempt to modify it as to allow for the inclusion of moral principles as a possible source of law, Austin suggests an alternative descriptive framework. While retaining the descriptive distinction between morality and positive law Austin suggests that morality is nonetheless a source of positive law, through positive law's connection with positive morality. Law as a whole is not only based in such a way upon morality but, more importantly, is made accountable to moral principles while continuing to be based in a clearly identified social source, the sovereign. I have said above that Hart could be thought to have moved jurisprudence away from Austinism's dominating idea of law as the product of political hierarchy and towards his own idea of understanding law through a hierarchy of conventional rules. It is of course beyond the scope of this article to develop a contemporary complementary theory of law along the lines of Austin's complementary jurisprudence, but consider this: It could be that a fresh understanding of Austin's notion of political hierarchy, based as it is upon morality, is the perspective needed to successfully supply the normative basis that some see Hart's account as lacking.

REPORT

REPORT ON THE 26TH ANNUAL INTERNATIONAL MEETING
OF THE AMERICAN MARITAIN ASSOCIATION

"Jacques Maritain and America"
Princeton University, October 17-20, 2002
Sponsored by: James Madison Program in American
Ideals and Institutions at Princeton University
Conference Chair: Christopher Cullen, S.J., Fordham University

The 2002 Twenty-Sixth Annual International Meeting of the American Maritain Association on "Jacques Maritain and America" at Princeton University could not have been more relevant to the current political climate, at least with regard to issues surrounding Church and State. The conference was held on October 17-20 and was sponsored by the James Madison Program in American Ideals and Institutions at Princeton University (Robert George, Director and McCormick Professor of Jurisprudence). The conference chair was Christopher Cullen, S.J., Fordham University.

But with well over 80 presentations, it is a very daunting task to try to report on it! Not being able to bilocate, I will attempt three things: to share just a few of the highlights that I experienced, to share some wonderful quotes—the conference was full of them—and to draw together some themes I saw emerging from the conference.

Douglas Ollivant (Command and General Staff College, Ft. Leavenworth, Kansas) gave a very informative and provocative talk about the philosophical background to just war theory and why we should support the Iraq war. We heard Richard John Neuhaus, Editor of *First Things*, on "Maritain, America, and the Paths of the Council" and David Schindler, Editor of *Communio* on "Thomism, America, and the Council" giving their very different visions about nature, politics and grace. We heard Desmond FitzGerald's fine presentation on the current popularity of Intelligent Design theory in his "Gilson, Darwin and Intelligent Design." We were treated to a performance of Gabriel Marcel's "The Lantern" (translated by Joseph Cunneen & Elizabeth Stambler and revised by Katherine Rose Hanley (a Marcel veteran who was present at the conference). We heard Paul E. Sigmund (Princeton) give an histori-cal/personal background to Maritain's teaching years at Princeton. Michael Novak (American Enterprise Institute) gave a very cogent argu-ment for the Judeo-Christian Tradition being at the root of our nation's identity in "Was the Founding Anti-Christian? Jacques Maritain on the American Founding." There was a bit of a feeding frenzy when Robert P. Kraynak of Colgate University arrived to defend his controversial but important thesis about the radical differences between genuine Christianity and the ideals of democracy in his book *Christian Faith and Modern Democracy*. There was worthy commentary on this by Jeanne M. Heffernan of Pepperdine University, John Hittinger of St. Mary's College of Ave Maria University and Richard Velkley of Catholic University of America.

There were some very some wonderful quotes that were shared throughout the conference. Regardless of how one might judge their over-all veracity, they are worthy of mention here. This conference had more meaty, pithy quotes than any other AMA conferences I have been to. Some of these were original to the speakers designated, others were passed on.

John G. Trapani Jr. (Walsh University) in his "Resolving the Tension Between Tolerance and Truth: Maritain on the Foundation of Democracy in America" said "Stress tolerance, you get relativism, stress truth alone, you get fanaticism." David Schindler proclaimed that "Relation is consti-tutive of the creature. So reason must be open to discovering the rela-tion—this is not gravy on the potatoes or icing on the cake! You can't basically know the creature where revelation is simply an addition." Desmond FitzGerald, while commenting on natural selection, said (and I tried to get the source of this but could not) that "Chance is the absence of explanation." Douglas Geivett of Biola University, talking about sci-entific naturalism and the Christian faith, said that "Stephen Pinker at MIT in his *Discover Magazine* article claimed that society had little effect on kids for they are hardwired. Notice the perfomatory contradiction!" Referring to McIntyre, Ralph McInerny offered this idea: "Speak from within a tradition and say so! Don't proclaim a view from nowhere. If a view is from nowhere, it has relevance to nobody!" Timothy Valentine S.J., on the similarities and differences between the educational theory of Maritain and Dewey, said "The problem of pragmatism is that it doesn't work!" Michael Novak of the American Enterprise Institute in the above mentioned paper wrote:

> To summarize: Jews and Christians conceive of the Creator as Spirit and Truth. The arena in which humans meet the Creator is, therefore, the inward conscience. The entire American theory of the foundation of natural rights hinges on this conception.

and

> William Penn of the Society of Friends first established religious liberty in the colonies and supplied the Christian rationale for it. In Penn's vision, Almighty God conceived of this universe we inhabit and brought it into being so that somewhere in it there would be at least one creature with whom He could establish friendship. And since God wished the friendship of free women and men, not slaves, He constituted human beings free. For Penn, friendship is the purpose of the universe, and friendship's necessary precondition is liberty.

"Fidelity only exists when it defies absence" and "It is through the individual, the concrete, that we reach the universal." said Teresa Reed (Rockhurst University) on Gabriel Marcel in her "Parts and Wholes in Marcel's Essays." Robert Kraynak defending his book *Christian Faith and Modern Democracy* (University of Notre Dame Press, 2001) proclaimed that "Democracy has nothing to do with Christianity" and the Church is like a "[W]oman riding a tiger. It ultimately eats her up...We are being swallowed up by 'rights.'"

We ended with a banquet where Michael Novak left us with these words, "We, each of us, were made for friendship with God...Democracy needs virtue, it needs God."

Finally, I wanted to say that here, more than in any other AMA conference I attended, many expressed views that were really opposed to another. These were not merely views one of which was the heroically good one, and the other a target, but really opposed views that created a cognitive dissonance in the group and demanded the participants to struggle to see and understand. There were no views that could be summarily dismissed. All had a cry, a call to arms, a painful nerve that needed to be addressed. Sometimes these tensions were embodied in the papers as it was for John Trapani's mentioned above in affirming both truth and tolerance or for Gregory Kerr's "Athens and Jerusalem in America" in affirming the tensions involved in theoretical, practical, and existential judgments involved in one's faith life. Other times, it was in the dialectical arrangements of the plenary sessions between Neuhaus and Schindler or Kraynak and his commentators.

This conference was the best in years, and they keep getting better. Keep your eyes on the lookout for the upcoming volume from Catholic University of America Press and, of course, come yourself to the next American Maritain Association Meeting! For more information, check out our Website at http://www.jacquesmaritain.org.

Gregory J. Kerr
DeSales University

BOOK REVIEWS

VIRTUE ETHICS: A PLURALISTIC VIEW
By Christine Swanton
Oxford University Press, 2003

Reviewed by Andrea Houchard
Department of Philosophy, Tulane University

While virtue ethics is typically understood as Neo-Aristotelianism, Swanton argues that such a conception unduly narrows virtue ethics in order to conveniently distinguish it from Kantianism and consequentialism: "As a genus, virtue ethics should be thought of as analogous to consequentialism, as opposed to, say, hedonistic utilitarianism" (1). Her pluralistic virtue ethics is not Neo-Aristotelian, though it draws on an Aristotelian notion of practical wisdom, a Nietzschean understanding of creative responsiveness, and an acceptance of Bernard Williams's claim that there is no single "right" or "best" response to many ethical problems. Swanton's account departs from other contemporary virtue-ethical theories by rejecting eudaimonism, though she does not deny that the virtues contribute to an agent's flourishing in many instances (62).

Virtue Ethics: A Pluralistic View is divided into four parts: Part I analyzes constitutive features of the virtues; Part II discusses common elements of all virtuous responses (universal love, self-love, universal respect, self-respect, and creativity); Part III details the dispositions of a virtuous agent; and Part IV gives an account of right action and explains how indeterminacy contributes to its pluralism. Swanton's treatment of the virtues in the first three parts grounds her conclusion that virtuous responses to particular situations allow for several "right" responses.

One of the most appealing aspects of the book—its pluralism—is also one of the most confusing, because the pluralism itself is plural. There are at least five ways virtue ethics may be plural:

(1) Items worthy of a moral response are plural;

(2) Virtuous responses to those items worthy of a moral response are plural;

(3) What makes a trait of character a virtue is plural;

(4) The standard for achieving virtue is pluralistic and contextual (i.e., does not require full excellence);

(5) Right action involves a pluralistic conception of rightness.

The spectrum of pluralistic elements is motivated by an attempt to deal with the complexities of real-world problems and contexts. It results in an account of right action that is "not too demanding" and according to which right actions may take various forms. Swanton's overarching objective is to rescue virtue ethics from criticisms that it fails to provide an adequate account of right action and is weak in applied ethics generally. Though she contends that a unity of the virtues prevents clashing or discordant responses, I will argue that the resulting portrait of the virtues is too loose to accomplish her avowed aim of strengthening applied virtue ethics. In order to make this case, I begin by briefly explicating Swanton's account of virtue and right action.

Swanton defines virtue as, "a good quality of character, more specifically a disposition to respond to, or acknowledge, items within its field or fields in an excellent or good enough way" (19). She describes it alternatively as a disposition to respond well to the "demands of the world" (21). These definitions are intended to be neutral between pluralistic and monistic accounts and do not commit her to eudaimonism, though Swanton offers additional arguments for why virtue ethics is plural and not necessarily eudaimonistic.

Since a virtue is a disposition to *respond*, Swanton begins by describing morally significant items that demand a response. These items comprise what Swanton calls the virtue's field: "The *field* of a virtue consists of those items which are the sphere(s) of concern of the virtue and to which the agent should respond in line with the virtue's demands" (20, emphasis original). Such items may be definitive, like money and environmental objects, or abstract, like honors, courage and beauty. A single virtue typically incorporates a heterogeneous collection of items in its field.

The various items in a virtue's field each have some basis of moral responsiveness: "A basis of moral responsiveness is a morally significant feature of the item responded to or acknowledged, and which at least partially grounds or rationalizes the form or mode of acknowledgement" (2). Swanton gives a non-exhaustive list of bases to illustrate the capacity of pluralistic virtue ethics to respond to morally significant items from a range of ethical theories. The bases may include value, status (acknowledging the Kantian emphasis on human status), good (acknowledging the consequentialist emphasis on promotion), and bonds (acknowledging human relationships and creativity). The virtue of justice, for example, is focused on honoring the rules of justice with respect for the status of individuals (22). So, any single virtue will have items in its field (such as honor and wealth) which create bases of moral acknowledgement (such as value or good) and such bases demand a virtuous response (such as appreciation or promotion).

Though there are many bases of moral acknowledgement, Swanton claims that all of them are related to the virtues. She rejects the theses of non-aretaic value and of value-centered monism. In her critique of the thesis of non-aretaic value, Swanton rejects the foundationalist picture advocated by Hurka and others whereby virtues are grounded in a list of primary goods. Her criticism of value-centered monism is largely a critique of consequentialism and what Swanton refers to as "the hegemony of maximization," but she also emphasizes that since the bases of moral acknowledgement are plural (with an emphasis on the bases of status and bonds), that any monistic account is thus refuted.

A basis of moral acknowledgement motivates a response. A "mode" is a form of response. Modes of responsiveness constitute a virtue's "profile," which is "that constellation of modes of moral responsiveness which comprise the virtuous disposition" (22). All profiles (and hence all virtuous responses) contain certain common modes: love, respect, expression, and creativity, which create a unity among the virtues. The "shape" of a virtue determines the moral standing required of a virtuous agent, and this in turn determines whether an action is "good enough" to meet the standard of virtue. That a response is required to be just "good enough" funds Swanton's threshold conception of virtue and contributes to the possibility of a plurality of virtuous responses.

To illustrate why different modes are required in a virtue's profile, Swanton considers the virtue of friendship. She follows Kant in interpreting love as an attraction that brings people together, while respect involves keeping one's distance. The virtue of friendship requires creative expressions of both love and respect, though different friendships require varying amounts of love and respect and various forms of expression. Swanton rejects grounding features for love and argues that a "range of virtues" may motivate love, given the incompleteness and complexity of human values and psychology.

By relating the virtues to human psychology and real-world contexts, Swanton limits the utopian ideals and perfectionism which are often associated with virtue ethics. She considers and rejects Rosalind Hursthouse's view that eudaimonism and naturalism can be combined in such a way to account for the full range of virtues. The worry is that Hursthouse's characterization of what it is to be virtuous *qua* human leaves out morally significant traits, and that an anthropocentric naturalism fails to explain why we must be responsive to the environment. Can we properly respect environmental objects or the status of animals when we focus on human-centered ends? Though the flourishing of natural systems and objects may not be good for humans *qua* humans, it may be indirectly beneficial. In fact, Swanton's account of objectivity, which emphasizes that we cannot totally escape our own subjectivism, seems to require that we value non-anthropocentric goods through an anthropocentric lens. Objectivity, on her view, demands not the absence of subjectivism, but rather the proper degree of it. Objectivity does not require a separation from the personal, since objectivity is a property of human agents (178-9). In part, these arguments for a subjective objectivity aim to alleviate concerns raised by Nagel in *The View from Nowhere*. As concerns environmental virtues, however, the implication is that we cannot appreciate nonhuman goods without accounting for our positioning in relation to them.

Another criticism Swanton makes of Hursthouse's naturalism is that, "A defender of virtue ethics need not be committed to a particular psychological account of character and what sustains it" (28). However, this claim is not adequately reconciled with the weak naturalism that Swanton accepts: "A correct conception of the virtues must be at least partly shaped by a correct conception of healthy growth and development which in part constitute our flourishing" (60). Indeed, it seems that any defender of virtue ethics must be committed to at least as much. But while this makes Swanton's pluralism more plausible, it is not easy to reconcile with her claim that an agent needs no particular character to be virtuous.

The last part of the book is devoted to developing a pluralistic conception of right action that is not tied to an ideal notion of a virtuous agent, again contra Hursthouse. Swanton focuses instead on whether or not an action comes close enough to a virtue's "target." This target-centered conception of rightness employs Aristotle's distinction between a virtuous act and an act which follows from a state of virtue. Hitting a target and performing an act from a state of virtue are virtuous in different ways. The target-centered approach exploits the profiles and modes of virtues so that a plurality of responses may be right: "A target may be reached in a minimalistic sense if an action is right but not right *tout court* (238)." Nevertheless, an action is virtuous in respect of a particular virtue if and only if it hits the target of, say, courage or generosity (228). This threshold conception of virtue allows varying degrees of the same sort of action to be virtuous. It does not require perfection or full excellence, and it also allows moral luck to contribute to rightness.

This account of right action may limit the force of the familiar criticism that because virtue ethics cannot determine *the* right action, a virtue-oriented approach is of little help in applied ethics. Swanton argues, however, that looking for a uniquely correct response to ethical dilemmas is misguided (274). The indeterminacy that arises in virtue ethics is a result of the fact that different virtues may point in different directions: perseverance and efficiency may suggest opposing responses, for example. Swanton thinks a dialogic approach will lead to an overarching principle, say, tolerance, that may account for both of them. If several different virtues apply to a particular situation, dialogue may lead to a position where, when all of the relevant constraints are considered, an overall virtuous decision may be reached. So too, unity among the virtues does not allow the indeterminacy to be excessive (286).

Nonetheless, Swanton's account seems too amorphous to be really useful in applied ethics. Swanton assumes there is no uniquely correct thing to do because there is indeterminacy among virtues. The virtues have complex profiles and virtuous individuals may respond to the same situation in different ways. Still, it would help if Swanton defined indeterminacy more precisely and made a more persuasive argument for it. A strength of her position is supposed to be that it makes virtue ethics more relevant to applied ethics, but just saying that any number of responses to a situation would be right does not supply the sort of guidance that applied ethicists typically seek. Indeterminacy, then, seems to undermine one of her avowed aims. Admittedly, her account still leaves open the possibility of a "best" response. The best response would not be required for an act to be virtuous or for an act to be performed from a state of virtue if virtue is a threshold concept.

Overlooking this difficulty, however, Swanton's account makes virtue ethics more flexible than it has previously been and also better able to accommodate the insights of other ethical theories. Her conception of "status-centered" virtue might make her account more appealing to those with strong Kantian intuitions, for example, and indeed Swanton claims that the differences between Kantians and virtue ethicists have been over-drawn (5). But the greatest attraction of her position is likely to be her pluralism. While virtue is paramount in virtue ethics, she leaves room for other normative elements, taking to heart Williams's observation that ethics should include many aspects of value, such as duty, status, good, and promotion, and not just one to the exclusion of the rest.

THE INVENTION OF AUTONOMY:
A HISTORY OF MODERN MORAL PHILOSOPHY
By J. B. Schneewind
Cambridge University Press, 1998

Reviewed by Jeffrey Downard
Department of Philosophy, Northern Arizona University

   J. B. Schneewind's aim in *The Invention of Autonomy* is to engage in a comprehensive study of the main currents of moral philosophy in the modern period. His reconstruction is guided by a number of commitments. First, he believes it is a mistake, and a fairly widespread one at that, to assume that the dominant feature of modern ethics is a move away from theological commitments towards an entirely secular ethics. Instead, Schneewind takes debates such as those concerning voluntarism and intellectualism, the relation between church and the moral life, and the respective roles of rational laws and the incentives of love to be central to modern ethics. While he believes the traditional distinction between empiricists and rationalists is not misguided, he chooses to organize his discussion along other lines. One reason is that Schneewind believes it is common for contemporary philosophers to assume that issues in epistemology and metaphysics are primary for most of the major modern thinkers, and that questions in ethics are only secondary in importance. This widespread assumption does not stand up to scrutiny, however, because most modern moral philosophers—including those who are today most famous for their work in epistemology and metaphysics— were as much moved by questions of morality, politics and religion, as they were by issues concerning the foundations of natural science.

   Having decided against setting up his discussion as a series of debates between empiricists and rationalists, it is necessary for Schneewind to use an alternate basis in organizing his discussion. The choice he makes is rather unique. What he thinks should be clear is the following general trend in ideas. In the medieval period leading up to Aquinas, the notion of what it was to be under a moral obligation was grounded on a model of obedience to God. Starting in many ways with Montaigne, there is a general trend to replace this model with an account grounded on the idea of self-governance. In the modern period, there are many different attempts to develop models of self-governance, but it is Kant who gives us what amounts to the most fully developed, and in many ways the most radical, account.[1] It is here, in Kant's account of autonomy, that Schneewind finds a basis for organizing his reconstruction of modern ethics.

Schneewind tells us that he was, at least in part, moved to engage in this rather enormous project by the following kind of question. In what ways was Kant's moral theory shaped by the philosophical debates that preceded him? Schneewind's hunch is that our understanding of Kant is in some measure hindered by the gaps in our understanding—as well as our misunderstandings—of these debates. For those who are especially interested in Kant's ethics, this book is a must read. But those who do not share this interest will be pleasantly surprised to discover that the richness of the story is not diminished by the choice of Kant as the perspective from which the tale is told.

One of the reasons is that this is not a history of ethics as it might have been told—with the benefit of much hindsight—by Kant himself. Nor is it a history that assumes Kant's theory is largely correct and views the preceding history as a series of steps as well as missteps that together lead us towards the truth. As Schneewind makes quite clear, he has serious reservations about Kant's account of autonomy. In fact, the choice of title is motivated by these reservations. He chose to refer to the work as the "invention" and not the "discovery" of autonomy because he believes Kant's account of autonomy has some serious problems. As Kant tells us, Leibniz invented the notion of a slumbering monad because the concept was not given to him but rather created by him. Similarly, Kant has created a particular conception of autonomy. Schneewind is not shy in telling us that there are three problems he finds particularly troublesome: Kant believes the idea of autonomy requires a notion of contracausal freedom; he believes our experience of moral obligation gives rise to a "fact of reason"; and he believes this experience shows us that we are members of a noumenal realm. Not surprisingly, these three parts of

---

[1] Stephen Darwall distinguishes several different senses of self-governance that he believes are not always kept clear in the text. See, "The Inventions of Autonomy," (On J.B. Schneewind's "The Invention of Autonomy: A History of Modern Moral Philosophy") *European Journal of Philosophy*, 7(3) (December, 1999): 339-350.

Kant's moral theory are troubling for many readers, including those who are more as well as those who are less sympathetic to his general point of view.

Using Kant as a frame of reference, Schneewind divides the discussion into four parts, followed by an epilogue. Having introduced the main themes that inform the work as a whole, he turns in part one to a discussion of the modern natural law tradition. In order to provide some background for those less familiar with this tradition, he begins with an overview of the origins of the natural law tradition and the development of the tradition in Aquinas. In addition, he provides context for the debates by introducing the arguments over voluntarism in Luther and Calvin. Schneewind's willingness to provide background and context for contemporary readers who find natural law theory foreign to their ears is indicative of the way Schneewind crafts the discussion throughout the work. Time and again, he turns to the central issues in politics, religion and science in order to provide a context, as well as some motivation, for the philosophical debates.

While he locates many of the debates in the larger context of ideas alive at the time, he also presents some of the debates in a more analytical fashion. When dealing with the question of whether or not God created what is good and evil, or whether they have a nature independent of the will of God, it matters not whether the debate is found on the pages of Plato, Aquinas or Leibniz because, in certain respects, the questions are timeless. I find this feature of the book especially attractive. Schneewind uses the best features of different historical methods and then weaves a coherent story that is more interested in the history of modern ethics than in debates about how that history ought to be told.

In the body of part one, he covers the natural law theories of Suarez, Grotius, Hobbes, Cumberland and Pufendorf and then ends with an account of the collapse of this tradition in Locke and Thomasius. In part two, he reconstructs modern perfectionist theories starting with Herbert of Cherbury and Descartes, moves to the Cambridge Platonists and ends with Spinoza and Leibniz. I find in this section two attractive features of the discussion that are indicative of what Schneewind consistently accomplishes throughout the text. First, his discussion includes what are often considered minor figures in modern ethics, such as Herburt of Cherbury, Benjamin Whichcote and John Smith, and the treatment of these "minor" figures is determined by a sense of what is important to the historical debates and not by a need to be encyclopedic. Second, the discussion includes major philosophical figures, such as Descartes and Leibniz, who are often ignored in discussions of moral philosophy. I came away from the text with a clearer sense of how the debates in epistemology and metaphysics between Descartes, Spinoza and Leibniz are shaped, in part, by their engagement with moral, political and religious questions. Given that Schneewind includes more than 80 figures in modern ethics, as well as several figures in ancient and medieval moral philosophy, it is no small accomplishment to craft a story that is so well told.

In the third section, Schneewind covers various attempts to develop a secular ethics, with responses from those committed to a closer connection between religion and morality. In this far ranging discussion, the debate starts with arguments between Gassendi, Nicole and Bayle, on one side, and Harrington and Shaftesbury on the other. As the debate takes shape, figures such Hutcheson, Butler, Hume, Reid, Bentham and de Sade take center stage.

In the fourth section, he focuses on some of the figures that more directly influenced Kant. The two German contemporaries that figured most prominently in Kant's own teaching and writing are Wolff and Crusius. From their theories, Schneewind turns to the debates between Le Mettrie, Diderot and Rousseau. In this discussion, he concentrates on the ways in which Rousseau's arguments formed an important turning point in Kant's reflections on ethics.

Up to this point in the text, Schneewind has devoted 21 of the 23 chapters to figures and ideas leading up to Kant's invention of autonomy. It is only in the last two chapters that he examines the various ways in which the debates in the history of modern ethics helped to shape Kant's moral theory. The reason he gives for moving so quickly through what could easily have taken hundreds more pages is that the main features of Kant's moral theory are so well known. Instead of attempting to provide a more comprehensive account of how Kant's theory was shaped by these debates, he chooses to focus on a part of Kant's ethics that has received less attention. According to Schneewind, one of the important breakthroughs that Kant needed in order to invent his concept of autonomy came in his early reflections on the problem of theodicy. In the rest of this review, I propose to examine Schneewind's account of this turning point in Kant's thought.

Most Kant scholars agree that a major turning point in Kant's thought occurred in the transition from his pre-critical to his critical philosophy. It is normally assumed that, in his ethics, this shift represents a movement from an ethics modeled on theories of moral sentiments, similar to what is found in Hutcheson, to an ethics grounded entirely on rational principles. According to Schneewind, this cannot be correct. The reason is that, in reading Rousseau, Kant saw a need to honor the common understanding of morality and came to agree that freedom must be the ability to give oneself the law. Furthermore, Kant indicates in his notes that the primary principle of morality must be a formal principle grounded on the non-contradiction of the will. Because these changes occurred quite early in Kant's thought, the transition from the pre-critical to the critical ethics must be more complex than is often assumed.

One of the important breakthroughs Kant needed to make sense of how a principle of non-contradiction could be grounded on the end of autonomy occurred in his early reflections on the problem of evil. Kant was drawn to this topic by a competition calling for essays comparing the systems of Pope and Leibniz. In a popular essay by Pope, he argued for the claim that all is good.[2] Leibniz denies this because it rules out the existence of evil. Leibniz attempts to make sense of the existence of evil in a world created by a perfect God in the following way. On his view, perfection is an objective characteristic of entities that is measured along two dimensions. First, the greater unity an entity possesses, the greater the perfection. Second, the greater number and diversity of entities brought into unity, the greater the perfection. Leibniz holds that the actual world is the most perfect possible world because there is no simpler way of bringing unity to a more complex set of entities.

The actual world contains evil for the following reason. God is in a position of examining the possibilities laid out before him and then choosing the best among the available options. God's choice of the most perfect possible world involves balancing the goods and evils of one possibility against the goods and evils of the other possibilities. God is not in

---

[2] Schneewind points out that this is Kant's understanding of Pope's thesis, and that his understanding is based on a poor translation of Pope's actual claim that everything that is, is right.

a position of determining what is possible. These possibilities are determined by the laws of reason. As an intellectualist, Leibniz rejects the claim that God can alter the laws of reason by a fiat of will.

On Kant's view, this is simply unacceptable. It is akin to saying that God desires the most perfect possible world, but due to constraints beyond his control, he can't have what he wants. Voluntarists reject this view because it makes God responsible for the choice of the evil that is in this world. Kant rejects the view because he believes it is incompatible with God's infinite perfection and independence.

As part of a strategy of defending Pope's thesis that all is good, Kant rejects two parts of Leibniz's account. First, he claims that perfection is not an objective feature of entities themselves. Rather, perfection is a relation between a will and what it brings about. Kant admits that this account of perfection is unconventional, but maintains that he has good reasons for insisting that the core of the idea of perfection always includes a reference to the will of a being endowed with cognition and desire. Second, Kant rejects Leibniz's account of possibility. On the view Kant entertains in this early essay, God not only determines what is actual, he also determines what is possible. To make what is possible independent of God's will is inconsistent with God's perfection.

I find it entirely plausible that shifts in Kant's thinking about such fundamental ideas as perfection and possibility were central in the development of Kant's mature moral theory. Schneewind offers a brief account of how these changes in Kant's thinking helped to bring this about, but the story he tells does not shed as much light as I would have hoped on the matter at hand. One of the problems Schneewind runs into is caused by his decision to focus on a limited part of Kant's moral theory. Having only a small part of the theory on the table, he seems to have insufficient conceptual resources with which to construct a plausible explanation. In one of the two chapters on Kant's ethics, Schneewind compares Kant's method in ethics to various methods philosophers might use in developing a moral theory. It is surprising that he says nothing about the transcendental method and how Kant uses it in developing his critical ethics.

The general idea behind the transcendental method is to use general logic as a basis for articulating the possible forms a synthetic judgment might take. The argument has the form of a regress: if the claims implicit in our common understanding of morality are legitimate, what would have to be the form and end of the primary principle of morality? Kant's argument works by a process of elimination. We assume that morality gives us overriding reasons to act, and that these reasons express themselves as moral obligations. Using general logic, we see that there are a limited number of possible forms the primary principle might have. In terms of the relation of the principle, it might be a categorical or a hypothetical imperative. In terms of its modality, it might be apodeictic, assertoric, or problematic. In terms of its quantity, it might be a universal, particular or singular. If morality is to give us overriding reasons, Kant argues that the principle would have to be a categorical imperative that is a universal and apodeictic law of reason.

Only after having established the form of the principle is it possible to determine its end. This is where many philosophers go wrong in their moral theories. They attempt to establish the end of morality first. One advantage of the transcendental method is that it enables us to see that only an end that is absolutely good could be the end of the primary principle. One conclusion that this argument is designed to establish is that certain types of formal principles, such as the principle of sufficient reason and the concept of perfection that it employs, could not be the primary basis of our moral judgments. It is the transcendental method that Kant uses in his attempt to show that the possibility of knowledge in morality—like the possibility of knowledge in natural science—cannot be grounded on the principle of sufficient reason.

What about the concept of possibility? Schneewind suggests that Kant was moved by problems of theodicy to rethink the assumptions behind Leibniz's account. But in the critical ethics, Kant is clear in maintaining that our understanding of morality can form the basis of a rational faith in God, and not vice versa. The ideas of autonomy, immortality and God are established only as practical postulates, and only after the transcendental analysis of moral judgment. Kant's argument for the postulates of immortality and God uses the following strategy. We take ourselves to be under a duty to perfect our virtue. The problem is that each of us would need an indefinite amount of time to accomplish this task. We also have to worry that nature—especially our own nature as beings with inclinations—makes it unlikely that the virtuous and not the vicious will turn out to be happy. If it is impossible for us to accomplish the goal of perfecting virtue or striving for a world where virtue and happiness are in accord, then we cannot be under such duties. Kant employs an 'oughts imply the relevant cans' strategy in legitimating the postulates. That is, if it cannot be shown on objective grounds that we are not immortal and that there is no perfect and infinite God, then we ought to assume for practical purposes that we are immortal and that there is such a God. It is only on the basis of such regulative ideas that we are able to live up to our obligations.

Kant needs to develop an account of possibility that is adequate to make sense of the idea of autonomy. The argument for the idea of autonomy is very different from the postulates of immortality and God. Schneewind seems to suggest that Kant's reflections about the nature of our immortal soul and the similarities between the human will and God's will help to shape his understanding of autonomy. I believe Schneewind needs to distinguish more clearly the question of how Kant might have arrived at the idea of autonomy from the question of how Kant attempts to justify the idea.

One striking point Kant makes that is not explored in the text is the claim that there is a significant difference between our will and God's will. On the supposition that there is a perfect God, we should assume that His will always does what is right. For God, the laws of morality are simply necessary. Human beings experience the requirements of morality as necessary requirements. But, insofar as we are free, we are capable of living up to the requirements or failing to do so. As such, for human beings, the requirements of morality are experienced as contingent necessities. What Kant needs is an account of possibility that is adequate to make sense of this special character of the human will.

As a whole, *The Invention of Autonomy* is a remarkable work. The unusual choice of using the perspective of Kant's account of autonomy helps to organize the discussion throughout. For those not particularly interested in Kant's ethics, it is possible to ignore the chapters on Kant and have a rich resource on the history on modern philosophy prior to Kant. For those who are particularly interested in Kant, Schneewind does us all a great favor, and the fact that he focuses on only a few issues that have received less attention in Kant leaves the rest of us plenty to do.

ALTERNATIVE CONCEPTIONS OF CIVIL SOCIETY
Edited by Simone Chambers and Will Kymlicka
Princeton University Press, 2002

Reviewed by Nicholas Hunt-Bull
Department of Philosophy, Southern New Hampshire University

This volume on civil society is part of the Ethikon Series in Comparative Ethics from Princeton University Press. It is organized as a discussion among scholars who act as representatives (some with slight embarrassment) of differing traditions in political theory. How, each was asked by the editors, does your tradition deal with ethical pluralism within a society? As Chambers and Kymlicka say in their introduction, "even the most homogeneous society will have to decide what is the right way of dealing with dissenting minorities and what are the boundaries of that homogeneity"(1).

The book opens with an essay by Adam B. Seligman that describes the historical development of the notion of civil society—those voluntary associations that fall between government and the family—in modern Europe. Seligman accepts the critique of liberalism made by Sandel and MacIntyre, finding in liberal theory a deep incoherence between its emphasis on individual rights and the morally legitimate demands placed on citizens by their particular communities. Nonetheless, "civil society" remains a potent phrase because it successfully picks out two distinct, although related, objects of discussion: in Eastern Europe, it represents an "institutionalization of those principles of citizenship upon which modern liberal democratic polities in the West are based"; while in the "West," it refers more specifically to the voluntary social institutions created by the associations, clubs, churches and political parties that citizens freely join (28). Robert Putnam, whose *Making Democracy Work* (1993) and *Bowling Alone* (2000) helped to popularize the term (and the related "social capital") is not a contributor to this volume, but casts an interesting shadow over it—while the authors discuss and analyze the expansion of democracy and civil society beyond its traditional home, Putnam famously warns us that it may be dying in the United States.

The nine essays that make up the remainder of the book (followed by an evaluative summary) fall into four circles which move progressively farther away from the central liberal tradition described by Seligman: closest is egalitarianism and "classical liberalism" (libertarianism); next come feminist and critical theory critiques of liberalism; the editors then move on to Christian thought in general and natural law theory; finally, furthest from the liberal consensus, and therefore most creative and interesting, are essays on the Jewish, Islamic and Confucian views of pluralism and civil society. Given the weakness that political theorists have for talking mainly within traditions, such a project that interweaves such a number of voices is highly refreshing.

Essays by Michael Walzer and Loren E. Lomasky introduce some of the central debates among contemporary egalitarians, liberals and libertarians. Walzer argues that associational life within society is essential, but requires protection and nurturing by government. He embraces civil society as a "school...for competitive coexistence and toleration, which is to say, for civility" (38). Emerging democracies need a vibrant civil society, Walzer notes, as a "'home' for oppositional tendencies and a guarantee that there will always be alternatives to any political establishment" (39). In a free society, citizens can freely choose to develop and define themselves through membership in groups and their projects. As societies have a tendency to reinforce existing advantages, Walzer argues that government should defend citizens' rights, and occasionally (as with the Civil Rights movement of the 1950s and '60s) intervene on the side of the weak. Lomasky, as our representative of libertarianism, endorses a minimal state, arguing that by contracting government and expanding the space of voluntary association we will enlarge freedom and opportunity. Moreover, humans are obviously social animals, so given free choice most of us will happily participate in group activities with others. We are not, in Lomasky's amusing phrase, "a collection of Garbos who want above all else to be left alone" (56). Those who do not participate in society may be miserable, but interrupting such misery does not justify violating their right to isolation or self-destructive stupidity. Unlike Walzer, Lomasky thinks that government should stay out of debates among associations that respect the minimal rights of others, and leave the success or failure of social experiments to the marketplace. Both essays are successful as exemplars of mainstream Anglo-American political theory at its clearest.

Representing the central views of one's traditions is much more challenging for the second group of authors. Anne Philips, in "Does Feminism Need a Conception of Civil Society?" takes on the formidable challenge of identifying a position that she can comfortably present as "feminist." She notes that feminists almost never mention civil society, except perhaps when noting the challenge that women face in achieving full citizenship. Otherwise, it "rarely figures in the feminist taxonomy" (72). Historically, male political philosophers like Locke and Hegel have interpreted the public sphere of civil society to exclude women. It was assumed that women deserved no public voice and belonged only in the non-voluntary sphere of the family. Yet, Philips acknowledges that the relative feminist silence in recent debates about civil society and social capital is surprising. Were not women central to the various group-based reform movements of the nineteenth and twentieth centuries? Philips explains this reticence by describing a fundamental disagreement between feminists and (mostly male) political theorists on where to draw the line between public and private: for the feminist, the politically interesting distinction is not between a public state and a private civil society, but rather between the broader public world of the state and civil society and the private space of domestic life. Thus, "boundary maintenance" between government and civil society, of the sort debated by Walzer and Lomasky, is of limited interest to most feminists (74). Further, given the successful feminist project of showing how family life influences our "public" lives, the notion of civil society can sometimes be stretched even farther, to include government, associations, and the family. Writing from a British and egalitarian standpoint, Philips notes that feminists are often right to suspect that public appeals to revive voluntary associations within civil society are coded references to shifting responsibilities from the state to individual women. "All too often," she writes, "this 'community' turns out to mean women, who are expected in their capacity as wives, mothers and daughters to resume responsibility for damaged members of the family..." (82). Philips thus endorses the European model of putting many responsibilities of maintaining the family (such as child care) into the hands of the welfare state, while respecting a plurality of voluntary associations, even religious ones that have problematic views of women.

Equally challenging is the task set to editor Simone Chambers, to provide "A Critical Theory of Civil Society." Discussing such authors as the Frankfurt school, Antonio Gramsci and Jürgen Habermas, Chambers explains that critical theorists exclude economic relations from civil society, since they see capitalism as at least as threatening to the values of free association as their traditional enemy, the state. The family, on the other hand, is included within civil society, since it plays a central role in the conditioning of citizens to accept the hegemonic ideological conformity of Western societies. The state, capitalism and civil society represent three distinct methods of social coordination, which privilege respectively power, money and communication. Habermas's goal is "communicative autonomy"—social and political freedom understood as the opportunity to participate in (partly idealized) communication and debate. Democracy is thus understood as the opportunity to take part in the public conversation that establishes public policy, rather than merely as voting and having rights. While constitutional rights are valuable, their value is not in protecting us from government coercion, but rather in letting us participate fully in social life. Such participation is threatened not only by totalitarian governments, but also by capitalist structures which seek to "colonize" civil society, for example by co-opting radical music to advertise products. In a surprising (but not expressed as such) return to Aristotle, Chambers sees a necessary connection between active participation in social/political life and full human autonomy.

Chambers and Philips both address the problem of "bad civil society"; that is, groups and associations like white supremacists that form associations which threaten civil society itself. Philips argues that feminism is stronger when it recognizes the need to avoid cultural imperialism, and so respects the *possibility* that veiled women in Islamic countries prefer to be covered. The recent political alignment of feminism and multiculturalism, however, creates unresolved conflicts. Chambers is less idealistic. Critical theorists, unlike many Americans, cannot ignore the danger that democracy (as in the Weimar Republic) can fall victim to associations (like the Nazi party) that develop under its protection. To her credit, Chambers does not offer any simple solution to the general problem of how to tolerate an intolerant, but she does argue that critical theory has a useful approach in seeking to "know why people join such groups in order to address the problem before it is too late"(103).

The third pair of authors, Michael Banner on Christianity and Michael Pakaluk on natural law, discuss the interaction between the liberal concept of civil society and Christian intellectual traditions. Banner explains that Christian social thought is rooted in Augustine's account in the *City of God* of the two cities, the city of God and the earthly city, only the first of which is truly a society. On Augustine's view, a merely earthly "society" is only a collection of competing individuals, since it lacks the shared love of God necessary for fellowship and peaceful co-existence. Such hostile coexistence of church and secular authority, Banner argues, was modified by Thomas Aquinas, who bridged the gap between the two cities by positing consistent teleological goals for the two spheres of life. Calvin, in contrast, sought dominance by the Godly over the secular rather than Augustine's independence of Church and Roman Empire. Historically, the Calvinist project of creating a richly pious society contributed, in that it encouraged cooperative institutions and associations in New England, greatly to the evolution of civil society in the modern sense.

Banner identifies two further concepts that Christianity contributes to the discussion of civil society: sociability and subsidiarity. Especially in its Aristotelian phase, Christian thought has emphasized the sociability of humans, our innate and natural tendency to group together and care for one another. For those who accept such a view of human nature, society cannot be the mere aggregate of selfish individuals posited by (uncharitably interpreted) liberalism. Catholicism also endorses leaving decision-making to the lowest level of a hierarchy of institutions that is competent to make it. This Roman Catholic doctrine of subsidiarity has been borrowed by the European Union in on-going debates about the appropriate relationships between individuals and levels of government (local, regional, national and Union wide). The Christian church remains a critic of liberal freedom, especially in its extreme form as laissez-faire capitalism, favoring goals of solidarity and personal salvation. Banner's essay is a rich and respectful effort to acknowledge the interplay of Catholic, Orthodox and Protestant thought, and the influence of thinkers from Augustine through Bonhoeffer and recent Popes.

Michael Pakaluk focuses his essay on natural law theory on the project of discovering what form of civil society natural law theory can endorse. He defines a minimal version of the natural law approach: that objective moral principles exist, and that positive law is legitimate to the extent that it conforms to those principles. Recognizing that such a minimal theory is insufficient to his project, Pakaluk adds two further assumptions, first that humans (and perhaps others) have certain essential properties, and second that the whole natural world has a certain systematic order. Given these assumptions, a society as interpreted by natural law will have multiple associations generated out of a network of duties and relationships, a self-regulating and "legally" governed hierarchy of communities. "The force of the law of political society," Pakaluk writes, "depends upon its recognition of the claims and duties constitutive of these associations, and the law of political society may, in some instances, lose its force if it contravenes these claims and duties"(134). Drawing on the Stoics, Scottish moralists and others, he identifies certain "modes of reasoning"—such as ideal type analysis and the use of analogies and "empathic reasoning"—that are characteristic of the natural law approach, arguing that even those who do not embrace the theory often reason in this naturalistic-teleological way. Natural law theories, which have limited numbers of followers today, seek to explain how and why we reason in such ways. Whether one accepts such an approach or not, Pakaluk suggests, one cannot escape thinking in the natural law mode and so being (perhaps) an unconscious adherent of natural law. Certainly most political theorists would agree with him that a precondition for successful democratic politics "is an extension to the political of a faculty for discernment that needs to be developed by practice in and appreciation of more mundane cases" (138). We need a civil society because participation in civil society allows the development of character and friendships that are central to a worthwhile human life. Unlike liberals or socialists, Pakaluk's natural law approach gives great authority to families and religions, noting that religion plays the social role of fostering "belief in claims of conscience that are prior to human convention or positive law" (141). Pakaluk's essay reflects the deep awkwardness of trying to fit the commitments of natural law belief within the political and social assumptions of modern liberal democracy. He endorses a role for the family incompatible with the individualism of our legal and social system, and a conception of freedom as constrained by "one's good" determined largely outside one's own choices. Even if, as he suggests, we are all natural law reasoners, many (myself included) will find even a modest natural law theory too tied to tradition, historical accident and socially imposed piety to be appealing.

The last section of *Alternative Conceptions of Civil Society* lives up best to the initial adjective of the title. Here three authors are challenged to find a place for civil society doctrines in traditions (Judaism, Islam and Confucianism) that have not included them. This is easily the most interesting and novel part of the collection, and it left this reader wanting much more, especially in its discussion of Islam. Suzanne Last Stone, in her essay on Judaism, notes that Diaspora Jews had little need for a theory of political society, since they mainly lived in communities separate from the dominant political societies they inhabited. This creates a significant challenge in modern times, since Jews must now make sense of religious pluralism in a state they dominate, Israel, rather than merely seek acceptance as a minority in another nation-state. Stone argues that the Biblical concept of the "resident stranger" who lives among the Jews while obeying basic laws has not yet been successfully stretched to accommodate modern notions of equal citizenship for all. Nonetheless, Jewish thought provides useful tools for a discussion of social solidarity and cooperation, including the Medieval thinker Menahem Ha-Ne'iri's thesis that Christians and Muslims can be recognized in a Jewish community since there are "lawful, disciplined societies" (157). The Jewish view of the individual is essentially community-related, since all members of the Jewish covenantal community share responsibility for one another and the following of the law as expressed in the Torah and commandments. Similarly, given the role of God and the law in every facet of life, Stone argues that Jewish tradition lacks the public/private distinction, multiple-spheres model, or concept of subsidiarity, central to civil society doctrine in Christian Europe. On Stone's account, Jewish thought does not treat sociality as a natural human trait, but rather as the product of law—social bonds are produced by culture and law, not human nature. While reason has a large role in interpreting the law, the law is given by God and not discovered by reason itself. Judaism has survived and prospered by maintaining certain traditions over many generations, traditions that are not wholly compatible with liberal civil society. Stone explains, "from within the rabbinic perspective, liberal civil society, defined as a realm of voluntary association and free entry and exit, is the problem of modern Jewish existence because it liberates individuals from the group, enabling them to discard traditional forms of life, express their identity in nontraditional terms, or put aside the question of identity altogether" (160). Liberalism sees competing associations as benign or even good, while many religions see them as a threat.

This is also noted by Egyptian philosopher Hasan Hanafi, who attempts the equally difficult task of negotiating a relationship between Islam and liberal pluralism. He suggest three models for this relationship: a rejection of civil society as a corrupt Western concept (as in Saudi Arabia, and in Afghanistan under the Taliban), an embracing of secular civil society as an alternative to Islam (represented in different ways by Lebanon and Turkey), or an attempt to find a middle way, which re-interprets Islam to find an balance between liberal rights and traditional Islamic law (as in Egypt, Jordan, and some of the Gulf states). Given recent American interventions in Afghanistan and Iraq, and the hyperpower's difficult relationships with much of the Muslim world, Hanafi's project is hugely important: "I believe that while the concept of civil society may be of Western origin, most of its key features may be found in Islamic ethical theory, and these features are slowly being realized in cultural contexts as different as the Moroccan and the Malaysian. Indeed, as I will argue...the development of this third approach to civil society—the reformist, modernist approach—is the only viable one for pluralistic Muslim societies, whether they are African, Asian or European"(172). Hanafi notes that civil society was invented in the West to allow a balance of powers within society, limiting the authority of kings and bishops. Similarly, in Islamic culture, the "umma" or community of all Muslims has variegated institutions, which divide powers. One notable example is the role played by religious scholars, whose interpretations of religious law constrain the actions of secular rulers. Even in medieval times, moreover, Muslim sovereignty allowed for the political status of Jewish and Christian subjects. Autonomous groups (*awqaf*) have long existed as scientific or literary societies endowed by donors and independent from the state. Although such groups were co-opted by the Egyptian government, their role in civil society has been partly re-invigorated by unions of lawyers and others affiliated with the Muslim Brotherhood. Islamic theory envisions an integrated religious/political society inconsistent with liberal notions of civil society, but it simultaneously endorses a diffusion of political and economic power consistent with the purpose of its invention in the West. Even if some fundamentalists have interpreted Islamic laws to treat non-Muslims as lesser citizens or tried to apply Muslim shari'a law punitively, Hanafi argues powerfully that such behavior is inconsistent with the elements of tolerance and fairness inherent in Islam. He is similarly critical of "theocratic authoritarianism" as practiced in Saudi Arabia or Morocco. He further argues that legal thinking analogous to the Western natural law tradition grounds an array of rights similar to those universally accepted, as in the United Nations's "Universal Declaration of Human Rights," but with a much lesser emphasis on private property and a much greater emphasis on redistribution of wealth than in the West. Hanafi sees himself as a participant in an ongoing debate between conservatives and progressives within Islam, with the former trying to impose a narrow and anti-liberal version of the faith, while the latter seek to revive the pluralism and intellectual fertility of early Islamic culture. As this debate goes on, Hanafi makes an interesting suggestion to his readers: "In both cultures, there is a certain imbalance between rights and duties. Muslim society may have duties without rights while Western societies may have rights without responsibilities. Islam needs a universal declaration of human duties to complete the Universal Declaration of Human Rights" (188).

Writing as a representative of Confucianism, Richard Madsen faces a similar challenge—to find a way to understand a central liberal concept that evolved from Western assumptions in many ways inconsistent with his tradition. The Chinese, he explains, did not even have a phrase translatable as "civil society" until the treaty ports, with their concessions reserved for Westerners, were imposed on them by the European powers. Contemporary Neo-Confucian thought draws on many traditions, including Buddhism, Daoism, and the authoritarian tradition of Legalism. Madsen restricts his comments to the "relatively liberal strands" of this complex tradition, on the grounds that this will allow at least some dialogue with Western customs. The challenge he faces is reflected in contrasting metaphors he offers for Western and Eastern views of persons: in the West people in society are like sticks bundled together in larger and larger bundles which remain individuals, in the East we are related to society like rings of ripples on a pond all overlapping and interacting. Distinctions such as that between public and private concerns, or the family and the society, are not firmly fixed. Madsen explains that "the New-

Confucian social order is based on the proper performance of interdependent social roles"(200). These roles are not chosen, but often assigned and involuntary. "For the Confucian," Madsen writes, "even voluntary associations, like learned societies or guilds, should be like families—their members should be bound by loyalties that make exit difficult" (202). Debates continue between scholars who follow Mencius in emphasizing the "five relationships" (parent/child, ruler/minister, husband/wife, older/younger siblings, friend/friend) of mutuality, and others who accept a Legalist interpretation of Confucianism that emphasizes the "three bonds" (ruler/minister, father/son, and husband/wife) of obedience. Madsen is clearly on the side of Mencius, but the Legalist approach clearly retains influence in China and Singapore. All traditions embrace an ideal of moral cultivation, which explains the long-established excellence of East Asian educational institutions, while strictly limiting the space for criticism of morality or state. States in the Neo-Confucian world impose laws restricting immorality and criticism, for example, that we would not accept in the United States. Even when, as in Taiwan, private associations of civil society emerge, they are regulated by the government. Modernization presents a great challenge to a tradition that emphasizes the slow and difficult cultivation of traits of character. Politics and economic exchange for Confucius and his followers was not, as many assume in the West, largely value-neutral. Morality and politics, like family and politics, are linked, which explains both the "crony capitalism" that many in the West complain about, and the difficulty Westerners have understanding the growing powers of East Asia.

The volume closes with an engaging summary essay by Michael Mosher, "Are Civil Societies the Transmission Belts of Ethical Traditions?" which begins with the sage comment that these are "daunting essays [that] combine reflections on civil society with an analysis of a fair sample of the world's ethical traditions" (207). Mosher argues, plausibly, that many of the authors accept too conservative a view of the role of civil society, assigning it the role of "transmission belt" of the dominant moral and political commitments of society, rather than as a source of truly independent voices that enrich and challenge society. In developing this argument, he attempts with limited success to find coherent themes in a rich plurality of essays. The difficulty of his task reflects the striking success of the editors in finding a group of intellectuals who genuinely and deeply disagree, and yet whose work interacts with and recognizes its opponents. It is a fascinating experience while reading this volume to find each author struggling anew to find a coherent account of, or response to, liberal civil society. This is the first book of a three-book series, and if the other volumes keep up the quality of work shown here, all three will become essential sources for debates about pluralism and democracy in the international community. You should read it and, if the circumstances permit, give it to your students—although challenging, the articles collected here give a rich introduction to traditions many students are unfamiliar with.

Adam Seligman notes in his introduction that many people in the ex-communist states of Eastern Europe, or we could add Iraq, have confused views about what civil society is, but clearly want more of it. Reading this volume of thoughtful political theory, we can see why, and perhaps even find tools to help them build greater freedom and opportunity for all.

BEYOND LIBERALISM AND COMMUNITARIANISM:
STUDIES IN HEGEL'S PHILOSOPHY OF RIGHT
Edited by Robert R. Williams
SUNY Press, 2001

Reviewed by Paula J. Smithka
Department of Philosophy and Religion,
University of Southern Mississippi

Beyond Liberalism and Communitarianism is an interesting collection of twelve essays addressing Hegel's political philosophy. It is an important addition to Hegel scholarship and a useful resource for scholars and students of Hegel's political philosophy alike. However, its utility could have been substantially enhanced with a more detailed index and a more comprehensive Introduction. Nevertheless, the text is innovative because Williams situates Hegel's political philosophy within the contemporary political debate between liberalism and communitarianism.

Political liberalism claims that individual rights serve as the foundation for a just state. The paradigm for a liberal state is that proposed by John Rawls in *A Theory of Justice*.[1] A liberal society is one where individuals have the maximum degree of liberty with like liberties for others, where the state is neither legally nor morally justified in using its coercive powers to undermine the basic rights of its citizens. Communitarianism, on the other hand, takes the welfare of the state to be primary and the rights of individual citizens to be secondary. This position is usually associated with Alasdair MacIntyre in *After Virtue*, and with Michael Sandel and Charles Taylor.[2] On this model, individual members of the community share an ideal for achieving the good life, or what Rawls calls a "comprehensive doctrine." The state is entitled to

[1] John Rawls, *Theory of Justice* (Cambridge, MA: Harvard University Press, 1971). See also his *Political Liberalism* (New York: Columbia University Press, 1993).

[2] Alasdair MacIntyre *After Virtue* (Notre Dame, IN: Notre Dame University Press, 1981); Michael J. Sandel, *Liberalism and the Limits of Justice* (Cambridge, U.K.: Cambridge University Press, 1975) and Sandel, ed. *Liberalism and its Critics* (New York: New York University Press, 1984); Charles Taylor, *Hegel* (Cambridge, U.K.: Cambridge University Press, 1975).

employ its coercive powers to keep members from threatening the shared ideal, because coherence and stability of the "community" are more important than individual rights. Hegel is more often associated with communitarianism than with liberalism, although the authors in Williams's text suggest that Hegel's political philosophy has liberal elements, primarily because a central concept in Hegel's political philosophy is the right to freedom. However, one of the goals of this anthology is to suggest that Hegel's political philosophy goes *beyond* either the liberal or communitarian approaches to a just state. In other words, Hegel's political philosophy is not reducible to either approach; instead, it achieves a synthesis, or an *Aufhebung*, of the two positions.

The main theme in Williams's book is the concept of freedom as a normative foundation for rights of individuals in their relationship to the state. Other issues in the book include postcolonialism, war, slavery, poverty, the relationship of one's body both to the self and to the state, social contract theory, and Hegel's political philosophy in relation to the views of Habermas, Foucault, and Rawls.

The first two essays discuss the normative foundations for Hegel's conception of Right and the State. Ardis Collins ("Hegel's Critical Appropriation of Kantian Morality") claims that Hegel himself explicitly accepts Kantian morality as the foundation of the concept of right. Collins's claims may seem surprising, but both philosophers accept individual freedom and reason as the subjective bases for objective morality. Thus, both agree that the good of the individual is tied to the good of the community and vice versa.

Kevin Thompson ("Institutional Normativity") claims that autonomy is the normative basis for rights. The civil society is just a larger version of the interdependent family model, where each individual has his/her own freedom. This makes Hegel's political philosophy sound very liberal, but autonomy only has full expression in civil society by attaining the good of the whole, which is more communitarian. Because the state has institutional authority to preserve and maximize the rights of individuals, an interdependence of citizens and the state is created to both support and reinforce the concept of right. It is primarily through the ethical existence (*Sittlichkeit*) of the people within the state that autonomy, free agency, rights of freedom concerning property and contract, and the "validity of rational will" can be recognized culturally and in legal statutes.

Violations of these rights of freedom constitute crimes and are punishable. What is interesting about Hegel's account of punishment is that the criminal has a *right* to punishment, as Dudley Knowles points out ("Hegel on the Justification of Punishment"). Knowles's essay is particularly interesting, because he claims that Hegel's justification punishment is a "near miss" of social contract theory. Hegel opts for the claim that engaging in criminal action generates an internal contradiction. The action cannot both be a right and a crime (132). Punishment of criminal actions is required for the restoration of right and must be a public function, but had Hegel adopted a hypothetical social contract model, all that would be required to punish a criminal is that he implicitly accepts the social contract concerning the rule of law, not that he actually consents to his punishment.

Apart from the ethical foundations of the state, what is it that binds free autonomous individuals together to form a community or a state? Mark Tunick rejects class, race, gender, ethnicity, common language, and other "ties that bind" ("Hegel on Political Identity and the Ties that Bind"). In order to identify the "body politic," Tunick filters Hegel's distinctions between a people (*Volk*), a state (*Staat*), a nation, and "communities." The state (*Staat*) seems to be the body politic for Hegel, but it is not identical with *Volk*, nation, or "communities." According to Tunick, Hegel seems to suggest geographic location has something to do with the ties that form a state, but that is not sufficient. Neither is the *Volk* the state (72-73). Sameness of language and religion might contribute to a *Volk*, but the ties that bind people together into a body politic also seem to include "shared accomplishments, memories, possessions, practices, and institutions." The people must share a common view of the ethical life (*Sittlichkeit*). Nations, on the other hand, may have several states. In the case of the Germanic people, the nation includes "Franks, Normans, English, Scandinavians"; or, they might be stateless. "Communities" seem to be groups of individuals that share some common practice, e.g., religion, but the state should tolerate a religious diversity (72-74). Hegel calls the state "our substance," and it is fundamentally important in achieving ultimate subjective freedom (83).

While Rawls makes a distinction between a moral identity and a public or institutional identity, it is not so clear that Hegel maintains this kind of distinction. In fact, it seems that he does not. The modern Hegelian state is supposed to be the embodiment of ethical life (*Sittlichkeit*), and people are amalgamated within the state. How is it then possible that moral and political identities remain distinct? It depends on what is meant by "amalgamation." While Tunick seems to suggest that this distinction is preserved, he admits that Hegel is not clear on the distinction between "amalgamation" and "assimilation," and Tunick doesn't say what he himself means by "assimilation."[3] Alan Patten ("Social Contract Theory and the Politics of Recognition in Hegel's Political Philosophy"), however, shows that the role of *Bildung* is extremely important for Hegel's state:

> *Bildung* is the term used by the German *Aufklärer* to designate both the process of education and acculturation that an individual or people must go through to achieve freedom and rationality and the result of the process...An individual undertakes *Bildung* in the schoolroom and at the knee of his parent or *précepteur*, but also, Hegel is claiming, in the broader context of his social, cultural, and even political experience. (172)

If this view of Hegel is correct, then the moral and political identity of the citizens of Hegel's modern state simply cannot be distinct, and so reflects a communitarian approach to society.

Stephen Houlgate ("Hegel, Rawls, and the Rational State") argues that Hegel and Rawls are more similar in their political approaches than what many people believe, thereby suggesting a more liberal Hegel. Rawls and Hegel agree on the importance of "individual liberty," and Hegel's political philosophy encourages tolerance for diversity, even though Hegel opposes "cosmopolitanism as an ideal." Furthermore, Houlgate claims:

> A rational modern state should rest on the broad foundation of Christian—preferably Protestant—belief, and the state, accordingly, may provide assistance to the church to further its

---

3 "Assimilation" often means an accommodationist approach to racial and/or ethnic integration. The commonly used metaphor associated with "assimilation" is "melting pot." Cultures and traditions are so blended together that they become indistinguishable, usually "accommodating" the desires of the race or ethnicity in social and political power. Booker T. Washington is often considered to be an assimilationist in the sense of being accommodationist. See *Up From Slavery*, (New York: Penguin Books, 1986).

religious ends. But Hegel also recognizes that individual citizens have the right to belong to whichever particular church community they choose...Thus, even though a modern state can incorporate non-Christian minorities, Christianity must predominate if the state as a whole is committed to freedom and right. (251)[4]

Notice that religious liberty is limited; it can only take place within the context of a predominantly Christian state, just as individual liberty is only maximized within the context of living the ethical life within the state. So, how is this "liberalism" at all?

While Hegel advocates a constitutional monarchy with a two-tiered parliament, the constitution of the state is essential, as Andrew Buchwalter points out ("Law, Culture, and Constitutionalism"). The constitution is linked to the *Volksgeist*, the spirit and identity of the people (213). The constitution both expresses the customs of the nation and serves as a means of self-definition or "collective self-interpretation" for the people (219). Buchwalter claims, "...the constitution is conceived as the organizing principle that sustains and indeed constitutes a people, the principle that both expresses and shapes its identity" (213). Having a monarchy is important, because a federal state is too unstable. With respect to America, Hegel writes in 1830 that, "it has not yet progressed far enough to feel the need for a monarchy. It is a federal state, but such states are in the worst possible position as regards external relations." In Hegel's view, federal states are too weak to hold together and would not attain the required recognition as a legitimate political institution by other states. Such recognition is more likely achieved in the form of a constitutional monarchy.

Hegel's state has two houses of Parliament. The upper house "should be reserved for members of the agricultural or landowning estate who inherit their property through primogeniture." According to Houlgate, these persons are the only ones who can guarantee their "political inde-

---

[4] According to Houlgate, Christianity alone "actively promotes the freedom of personality."

pendence," and ideally must participate in working the land in some way
(257). The second tier of Parliament is comprised of representatives of
corporations (*Korporationen*). Corporations are not instantiations of a
planned economy per se, rather they are institutional associations based
on the guild system that govern the production and consumption of products within a state. In a completely free market society, Hegel thinks that
without corporate governance, a state would either be over-producing or
under-producing goods and services. Corporations (not states) regulate
production and consumption by limiting the number of workers who can
produce various products, since the goal of corporations is to maximize
overall economic welfare for the state (254). In an Hegelian parliament,
the representatives of these corporations are to keep the best interests of
the general working citizenry in mind. Houlgate states, "...the stability of
the modern state rests partly on the trust that citizens have that their particular interests are indeed protected by the state, [and] it is essential that
the interests of the various trades and professions to which citizens
belong be seen to be represented in the legislature" (255).

Houlgate and Joel Anderson ("Hegel's Implicit View on How to
Solve the Problem of Poverty") both address the governmental structure
of the Hegelian modern state as it pertains to power and wealth. Houlgate
readily admits that Hegel is less "democratic" than Rawls, but maintains
that both Rawlsian and Hegelian modern rational states are the same *kind*
of state; namely, "a liberal modern state governed by laws and principles
of justice that are recognized as binding by all free and rational citizens"
(252). Anderson maintains that Hegel's concern with the good of society
is reflected in Hegel's claims that the state should recognize that there is
an appropriate standard of living for its citizens. But the state's standard
of living and its economic stability are largely in the hands of corporations. "Hegel seems to favor a familiar welfare package including public
provision of minimal needs, assistance in locating work, and job training
and education, especially as these are provided through the *Korporation*"
(190). Should corporations fail to maintain a stable society, the masses
will fall into poverty. The problem is with coordination of production and
consumption. Consumption must be done responsibly and so spending
money "becomes an ethical matter" (192-194). A stable Hegelian economic society is one that will supposedly maximize employment and production opportunities without straining the markets so as to avoid creat-

ing impoverished conditions. Impoverished conditions may concentrate wealth in the hands of a few and generate a "pernicious rabble." But Hegel's primary concern with poverty seems to be that this rabble would destabilize the state. In other words, the community is primary, and the well-being of poverty-stricken individuals is of secondary and derivative importance. This suggests stronger communitarian, rather than liberal, leanings.

Richard Dien Winfield's essay ("Postcolonialism and Right") addresses the problems of modern states, which were largely developed on the basis of ideals of freedom and self-determination, but which tend to view other societies, cultures, or states as "premodern." Can a modern state, like that advocated by Hegel, legitimately impose modernization on premodern societies? As Winfield asks, "Can communities be compelled to be free?" (98). This is an important question, considering the recent wars in Afghanistan and Iraq. While Kant thinks that any such imperial domination is unjust, Hegel and Mill provide a justification for it. For both of these philosophers, colonialism offers the opportunity for participation in the fundamental right of freedom. Inconsistent though this may seem, Winfield sees the potential outcomes for postcolonial areas positively, since modernity has "embraced freedom." Because an Hegelian modern state takes political freedom to be an end, Winfield claims that two normative challenges arise for the colonizers with respect to the colonized: "(1) the colony must be transformed into a province of the metropolitan nation, with the same political participation as any other, or (2) the colony must become an independent democracy" (102). The first seems to require assimilation (amalgamation?) of the colonized, while the second requires the colonizers to be willing to give up their political power in favor of the ultimate right of freedom. Winfield takes the more optimistic view that postcolonial independence, if modeled on Hegel's modern state with the right of freedom and the basis of the ethical life, will ultimately be a "harbinger of political self-determination" (106).

Since one reason for colonization was to provide more resources and markets to satisfy the needs of the state, I am not convinced that Hegel's modern state would be so willing to grant political self-determination. Letting go of colonial resources and markets might actually destabilize the state, which would be unacceptable to Hegel. Maintaining a stable state recognized by others as economically and politically powerful might be enhanced by having colonies. Should the colonists create instability, then the colonized nation might be granted independence. However, the more pressing moral issue has to do with the justification of colonization and the issue of assimilation (amalgamation?). Even if Winfield is correct that an Hegelian modern state would grant political freedom to a post-colonial nation, Hegel, and some of the essays in Williams's volume, suggest the state has priority over civil society. Even though colonized peoples may be considered to be a "community," much of their own cultural practices would be erased.

This concern is supported by Buchwalter's argument that Hegel's approach to law is "culturalist." The law and the constitution of the state do not address political concerns of the state alone; rather, they embody and define social practices and norms. Buchwalter claims, "...Hegel's position furnishes the parameters for a normative account of the reproduction and self-production of a culture" (220). The role of educational institutions together with disciplinary institutions such as the Polizei have the goal of "erecting the sociocultural hegemony of ethical life over the individual which...augment the negative or repressive interventions of the state by cultivating in individuals interests that promote their more habituated, normalized, and 'spontaneous' support for the state," according to David Durst ("The End(s) of the State in Hegel's *Philosophy of Right*") (239). So, the right to freedom of the individual is secondary to the right to freedom for the state. In the case of colonization, the "community" of the colonized's rights to freedom would also be secondary to the right of freedom of the colonizing state.

While on the surface, Hegel supports a kind of political liberalism, upon closer inspection, the unity of the state is the primary concern. This unity depends upon maintaining a "shared vision," or "comprehensive doctrine," of the state. It is precisely the lack of such a shared vision, according to Stephen Stepelevich ("War, Slavery, and the Ironies of the American Civil War"), that caused the American Civil War. He claims that the United States then lacked a "fixed national identity and a unifying moral aspiration" (148). The lack of this shared vision suggests just how significant the "collective self-interpretation" of people is for Hegel. It appears that political identity and moral identity are entirely interwoven in the ethical life of the state. Without a free state, individuals cannot fully realize their own individual freedom. This also lends support to the claim that Hegel is more communitarian than liberal. Thus, while Williams and some of the authors in book claim that Hegel has offered an *Aufhebung* to liberalism and communitarianism, I remain unconvinced. Nevertheless, *Beyond Liberalism and Communitarianism: Studies in Hegel's Philosophy of Right* is an interesting and important addition to Hegel scholarship and his political philosophy.

THE ENCHANTMENT OF MODERN LIFE:
ATTACHMENTS, CROSSINGS, AND ETHICS
by Jane Bennett
Princeton University Press, 2001

Reviewed by J.N. Johnstone-Yellin
University of Idaho and Washington State University

Drawing upon writers as diverse as Paracelsus, Marx, and Thoreau, Jane Bennett, in *The Enchantment of Modern Life*, creates a text that is initially intriguing. Arguing that we cannot expect a society disenchanted by postmodern cynicism to perform ethical actions, Bennett advances the "affective force" of moments of enchantment as a source of energy that might "propel ethical generosity" (3). However, no matter how interesting and engaging her text is, she fails to deliver what she promises. Rather than a sharp and insightful exposition of her thesis, Bennett is content to ramble through her 'alter-tale'[1] sharing stories that fail to advance her argument.

In an attempt to understand Bennett's thesis, the reader must consider what she means by "enchantment." It is also important to consider her contention that one can be enchanted by commodity culture. Using Bennett's definition of "enchantment," I argue that while one may be enchanted by commodity culture, as she maintains, Bennett fails to elucidate how that enchantment results in ethical action.

OVERVIEW

Summarizing Bennett's book is not an easy task. She does not build her argument from chapter to chapter, but instead introduces a vast array of thinkers and ideologies that are intended to support her various descriptions of "sites" of modern enchantment. Also, Bennett is not trying to create a new account of enchantment, but is instead attempting to persuade her readers to resist the story of the disenchantment of modernity. As a result, a brief synopsis will not adequately reflect Bennett's

---

[1] Bennett defines 'alter-tale' as an alternative narrative discussing anti-disenchantment with an otherwise disenchanted society.

text, but it will indicate the diversity of the thinkers and ideologies that she discusses.

After introducing her project, Bennett articulates "an ethical sensibility that is extended to nonhumans as well as to humans" by considering "cross-species encounters" (13). She then moves on to consider Paracelsus's outdated teleological model of enchantment. Paracelsus's world is one of "divine prose," she tells us, while Kant "invents an amazing interior world of reason" (13). According to Bennett, it is important that those of us in modernity realize that enchantment was not only a feature of medieval or Renaissance times, but that it also can be found in contemporary life. Only when we realize that enchantments exist all around us will we begin to notice them.

In the fourth chapter, Bennett introduces her reader to the disenchantment tales of Weber, Blumenberg and Critchley. In response to these thinkers, Bennett claims that even if the world is calculable, modernity is secularized, and we are pursuing an ethics of "finitude," it is still important to draw enchantment from science, reason and other calculable paradigms. The book's most interesting chapter draws upon Thoreau, among others, to develop an "enchanted materialism, an onto-story of matter that is lively and wondrous but not necessarily part of a divine creation" (92). She then investigates complex, technological sites of enchantment before concluding that a Kafkaesque encounter with the highly complicated and intricate web of bureaucracy could provoke a sense of enchantment.

Bennett continues with an investigation of Marx's notion of "commodity fetishism," examining whether we can be enchanted by commodities and commodity culture. No matter whether commodity enchantment takes the form of sights, sounds, or something completely different, Bennett argues that without enchantment, "we might not have the energy and inspiration to enact ecological projects, or to contest ugly and unjust modes of commercialization" (174). Finally, her text concludes with a chapter on enchantment's connection to æsthetic disposition and moral sentiments and a chapter that positions her 'alter-tale' in relation to Stephen White's notion of weak ontology.

Given the density and scope of the material that Bennett covers, it is difficult to discern a clear thesis from her text. One must consider each thinker, each ideology, and each contradiction before concluding how each component shapes her overall project. Nonetheless, a recurring problem involves what she means by 'enchantment.'

A PHENOMENOLOGY OF ENCHANTMENT

Initially, Bennett's use of "enchantment" seems rather straightforward and uncomplicated. "To be enchanted is to be struck and shaken by the extraordinary that lives amid the familiar and the everyday" (4). However, a few paragraphs later Bennett introduces a more mystical definition:

> ...*enchantment* entails a state of wonder, and one of the distinctions of this state is the temporary suspension of chronological time and bodily movement. To be enchanted, then, is to participate in a momentarily immobilizing encounter; it is to be transfixed, spellbound. (5)

Surprisingly, Bennett's mystical definition appears in a text that attempts to bring modernity closer to a state of enchantment. In turning to the mystical, Bennett creates a definition that would limit the number of people experiencing enchantment. This is contrary to the general connection she tries to draw between enchantment and everyday ethical action.

One reason for Bennett's move toward the mystical could be that her simple definition leaves enchantment open to the charge of naïve optimism:

> It raises the question of the link between enchantment and mindlessness, between joy and forgetfulness... I do not deny such a link or its dangers, but I also argue that, in small, controlled doses, a certain forgetfulness is ethically indispensable. (10)

Clearly, "forgetfulness" and "ethically indispensible" reflect a problematic use of language on Bennett's part. Rather than clarify the meaning of each, she instead clouds the matter with an endnote. Using a point similar to that made by Wendy Brown in *States of Injury* (Princeton University Press, 1995), Bennett explains that the forgetting of which she speaks is something of a Nietzschean "forgetting," where one has invested so much in one's history of suffering that one must forego the investment "in pursuit of an emancipatory democratic project" (176). It appears then that we are faced not with a naïve forgetfulness, but instead a psychologically rich forgetfulness, a forgetfulness necessary for our future enchantment. Without such forgetfulness, she suggests, our future holds only disenchantment.

Why? Bennett is unclear on the point and simply leaves her use of "forgetfulness" for the reader to interpret. Unfortunately, she leaves the reader so few clues as to what she means that her point becomes lost if not absurd. Should we, for example, "forget" the ecological damage that humankind has wreaked upon the planet? Surely such "forgetting" would lead humankind to repeat mistakes of the past. Further, are we to conveniently "forget" about the starvation, war, and disease we witness on the evening news, so that we can better focus on the enchantment that resides in the commercials in between? How can "a certain forgetfulness [be] ethically indispensable" (10)? Without further elucidation, her advice appears both ridiculous and contrary to her stated ends with regard to ethical action.

COMMODITY FETISHISM

Bennett's portrayal of commodity fetishism is one area of her text where she is undoubtedly conflicted. Although sympathetic to modern critiques of capitalist structures, Bennett responds to Marx, Horkheimer and Adorno's discussions of commodity fetishism in an attempt to portray a modern television commercial as a source of enchantment. The conflict lies, as we will see, in Bennett's inability to successfully defend, or even successfully explain, the juxtaposition that allows one to be enchanted by a commercial without experiencing disenchantment because of a company's capitalistic and unethical practices.

In "Commodity Fetishism and Commodity Enchantment," Bennett argues that television advertisements can enchant society. She describes in great detail a single advertisement, "Khakis Swing" by GAP, which aired in 1998. Suffice it to say that this ad features a mix of male and female dancers all wearing GAP khakis. While Louie Prima wails in the background, the camera freezes the closest dancer in mid-flight before panning wildly around the room. Bennett sees the room spinning and swinging as if it were one of the dancers. She explains:

> I position this GAP ad, wherein the room and the khakis dance
> along with the human bodies in them, in a tradition of works
> of art that explore the phenomenon of animation—of dead

> things coming alive, of objects revealing a secret capacity for
> self propulsion. (113)

While Bennett sees only commodity enchantment in "Khakis Swing," the
reader should also consider the presence of commodity fetishism and
what that means for the enchantment of modern life.

Early on, Bennett writes that "sites of enchantment today
include…the animation of objects by video technologies" (4), but later
asks whether we can be enchanted by "animations designed to make [us]
purchase something" (112). She argues that, "enchantment, from multiple
sources, can be used to feed or fuel an ethical will" (114). It is problematic that Bennett does not say whether all sources of enchantment are
good, or lead to good actions. However, given the source of her example,
it would appear that no matter how ethically bankrupt the source, the
value of the enchantment lies in the product itself. So long as we are
enchanted by the GAP advertisement and ignore the fact that GAP has, in
the past, been charged with violating human rights and boycotted by
PETA for its poor animal rights history,[2] then our enchantment will lead
to ethically sound actions. This type of "forgetting," however, does little
to advance Bennett's project.

Bennett claims that she wants to "extract the ethical potential within
commodity culture" (113), telling her reader that:

> Ads have tended…to inculcate on the senses—to write into the
> body—an aesthetic image of the slim, beautiful (male or
> female) body. Demystification is indispensable as a counter to
> this normalizing power. (113)

And yet, according to Bennett, if the technology captures our imagina-
tion, if the soundtrack can stop us in our tracks, or if we allow ourselves
to be mystified, then an advertisement is enchanting—no matter the body
image presented and the message sent out by the advertisers. Once again,

2 In January of 1998 (the year of GAP's "Khakis Swing" advertisement), Global
Exchange (a national human rights organization) filed a $1 billion lawsuit against eigh-
teen United States retailers, GAP included, charging the companies with violating basic
human rights. In 2000 PETA (and Chrissie Hynde) protested the use of leather from animals killed in India and China. These are two countries where, among other cruelties, wit-
nesses have observed cows being skinned while slowly dying from having their throats
slit.

the reader is left to ponder the tensions in her argument. Bennett continues to write:

> Commodity fetishism is a kind of perceptual disorder. Humans become blind to the pain and suffering embedded in the commodity by virtue of an unjust and exploitative system of production. (113)

Ironically, this statement could describe the ways in which a GAP commercial can enchant. To be enchanted by "Khakis Swing" is to be blind to the sweatshops and animal cruelty behind GAP commodities.

How could being enchanted by a commercial lead one to act in a more ethically sound way? Would it not be ethically sound behavior to boycott GAP until it ceases its use of sweatshops, rather than rush out and buy a pair of GAP khakis? The problem appears even worse when Bennett claims that she:

> ...explores the ethical substance internal to the style of the ads. That the style can be described as an aesthetic of vibrant mobility, of the ever-present possibility of bursts of vitality that violate an order ranking humans incomparably higher than animals, vegetables and minerals. (114)

Clearly, GAP advertisements do not violate the order Bennett mentions, and so it is unclear how they contribute to the sort of paradigm shift Bennett expects to arise from commercial enchantment. GAP continues to uphold the order, unconscionably placing humans at the very top and abusing all other forms of life for its own ends. Where is the ethical action in all of this? Indeed, where is the enchantment?

In response to the first question, Bennett refers to the work of Horkheimer and Adorno. In a telling passage she writes that for these authors, "to say 'Yes' to pleasure is to say 'No' to critical thinking" (128). Without agreeing with Horkheimer and Adorno entirely, they seem closer to the truth than Bennett when she writes:

> Although pleasure can entail stupidity, passivity, and, eventually, moral indifference, I contend that it can also enliven, energize, and, under the right circumstances, support ethical generosity. (128)

Bennett never explains why pleasure (or for that matter, whose pleasure or which pleasures) will have these salutary effects. As she proves throughout, she has the skill to lead the reader towards a resounding crescendo but time and again fails to hit the right final note. When it comes to demonstrating the connection between being enchanted and acting ethically, Bennett continually fails to deliver. The closest Bennett comes to explaining this connection is when she writes:

> ...part of the energy needed to challenge injustice comes from the reservoir of enchantment... For without enchantment, you might lack impetus to act against the very injustices that you critically discern (128).

Still, how enchantment provides the energy for ethical activity is left unexplained.

On the whole, Bennett's "alter-tale" is an interesting journey that cuts a wide swath through the history of Western thought, and is the sort of text that one can enjoy over the course of a weekend. However, while this breadth of material makes for an interesting read, it also makes for a flawed piece of philosophy. With so many thinkers under consideration, no individual receives the attention necessary to sustain the argument. Perhaps Bennett should concede that in a disenchanted world, we cannot adequately express the meaning of "enchanted." We can only approach the subject as she has, by approximation or through metaphor. Perhaps her project is necessarily flawed as it attempts to move beyond logic and logos while avoiding the discussion of mysticism as faith. Still, reading *The Enchantment of Modern Life* can be worthwhile, as long as one does not expect an answer as to how the enchantment of modern life leads to ethical behavior.

CONTRIBUTORS

Lori Alward is an assistant professor of philosophy and environmental studies in the Department of Philosophy and Religious Studies at Pace University in New York. She received her M.A. and Ph.D. from the University of North Carolina at Chapel Hill. Her research interests include Kant, ethics, feminist theory, and environmental philosophy.

Avner Levin teaches at the University of Toronto. Mr. Levin specializes inWestern jurisprudence and has a growing interest in the thought of Austin.

Nancy Snow is an associate professor of philosophy at Marquette University. She received her M.A. from Marquette University and her Ph.D. from the University of Notre Dame. Her research interests include ethics, social and political philosophy, and philosophy of law.

Shelby Weitzel is an assistant professor of philosophy at College of the Holy Cross in Worcester, Massachusetts. She received her M.A. and Ph.D. from the University of North Carolina at Chapel Hill. Her research interests include ethics, political philosophy, feminist theory and environmental philosophy.

CALL FOR PAPERS

"Medieval Philosophy & Natural Law"

Vera Lex, the Journal of the International Natural Law Society, is currently seeking papers for a special issue devoted to "Medieval Philosophy and Natural Law."

The Middle Ages enjoy a prominent place in the history of natural law theory. *Vera Lex* invites papers that explore all aspects of medieval natural law theory, from its role in medieval ethical or political thought to its metaphysical implications and the epistemic status of its precepts. Papers dealing with Thomistic natural law are welcome, though studies of thinkers outside the Thomistic tradition (e.g., Scotus, Ockham) are of particular interest.

Deadline for Submissions: June 15, 2004

Submission Guidelines: Papers should be double-spaced and between 4000 and 8000 words in length. Two copies of the manuscript should be submitted to:

Mark D. Gossiaux
Department of Philosophy
Loyola University New Orleans
New Orleans, LA 70018

Additional questions may be addressed to
gossiaux@loyno.edu

CALL FOR PAPERS

"Natural Law"

We are issuing a general call for papers on topics in natural law. In the past *Vera Lex* has published articles on such topics as reason in natural law, natural law and constitutionalism, rights, equity, dignity, property rights and natural law, jurisprudence and natural law, legal positivism - natural law debate, pragmatism and natural law, autonomy, liberty, the Spanish, medieval and Hebrew tradition in natural law, and environmental philosophy and natural law. We also welcome papers on specific thinkers like Hugo Grotius, Giambattista Vico, Thomas Aquinas, John Locke, Thomas Hobbes, Edmund Burke, Thomas Hutchinson, John Stuart Mill, Lon Fuller, H.L.A. Hart, etc.

Deadline for submission is June 15th, 2004.

Please address all manuscripts to Editor, *Vera Lex*, Pace University, Department of Philosophy & Religious Studies, 41 Park Row, New York, NY 10038.

We are planning two "special issues" in the coming year: the new natural law system of John Finnis; "Medieval Natural Law and Application." If you are interested in submitting a paper or would like further information you can write to the Editor at the above address or e-mail rchapman@pace.edu

Environmental Values

EDITOR:
Alan Holland
Dept. of Philosophy, Furness Coll.,
Lancaster University, LA1 1YG, UK

ASSOCIATED EDITORS:
Michael Hammond
Lancaster University
Robin Grove-White
Lancaster University
John Proops
University of Keele

REVIEWS EDITORS:
Clive Spash
University of Cambridge
Jeremy Roxbee-Cox
Lancaster University

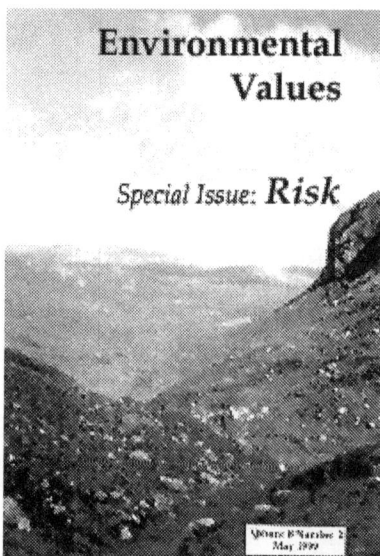

Environmental Values

Special Issue: **Risk**

ENVIRONMENTAL LAW is concerned with the basis and justification of environmental policy. It aims to bring together contributions from philosophy, law, economics and other disciplines, which relate to the present and future environment of humans and other species; and to clarify the relationship between practical policy issues and morefundamental underlying principles or assumptions.

The White Horse Press, 10 High Street, Knapwell, Cambridge CB3 8NR, UK
ISSN: 0963-2719 Quarterly (February, May, August, November)
Vol. 9, 2000, 144 pages per issue. Includes annual index.

Institutions: (1 year) £96 ($155 US)   ☐

(Institutional Rate Includes ELECTRONIC ACCESS)   ☐

Individual (1 year) £40 ($65 US)   ☐

Student/unwaged (1year) £30 ($50 US)   ☐

www.ingramcontent.com/pod-product-compliance
Lightning Source LLC
Chambersburg PA
CBHW021601210326
41599CB00010B/538